LETTERS TO MY SISTER

2017 Chadia Mathurin
Cover Design by Chadia Mathurin
Interior Layout by Heaven Dzign

Published by Wakonté Publishing
Wakonté Publishing is a subsidiary of Wakonté Inc.

Identifiers

ISBN 13: 978-1-947923-00-3 - Paperback

To My Sisters Who Endeavor To Read This,

When I first started writing these letters, I wrote them being careful to distinguish my writings for men and for women. I wanted two different books and if I am to wallow in truth and transparency, I think my desire stemmed from my hurt.

I wanted to ostracize men as I felt they had ostracized women. I wanted to band against them as I felt they had banded against us. I wanted to hurt them as they had hurt us. I wanted to marginalize them as I felt that they had marginalized us. I wanted to limit them as I felt that they had limited us. But as I wrote, I began to make discoveries.

I discovered that our destinies - men and women - are intertwined. I discovered that the fullness of humanity cannot be grasped without the harmony of man and woman. And because of these discoveries, I felt that each of these compilations - while each speaking in specificities to our burdens, our habits and our purposes - must seek to render a harmony that captures the fullness of His image and likeness.

I went back to the drawing board. I went back to figuring out how I could fully capture these things. My answer was to break the band of separation that the imperfections of our humanity have created. My answer was to not spend so much time "angelizing" womanhood while I "demonized" manhood. My answer was to provide a balanced view of our humanity: the good, the bad and the ugly; my answer was to address these issues in truth.

So sister, I write these letters to you hoping that you are encouraged, empowered, comforted, chastised, disciplined and discipled. I write these letters hoping that you will learn to love you and see the wisdom and purpose in God's design that is womanhood. I write these letters praying that you are inspired to aspire to the best version of you.

And I look forward to all the laughs, tears, disagreements and deep moments of reflection that are sure to come from your letters to me.

Oh. Feel free to shoot me a message asking me what the few sprinkles of Kwéyòl across the pages of this book mean. I'd be happy to indulge you.

Your Sister,
Chadia

THE
GIST

I AM
WOMAN.

Dear Woman,

As we begin this journey of swapping stories, experiences, triumphs, loves, dislikes, annoyances and hurts, I feel compelled to open with a letter weighted in transparency.

I have a beautiful younger sister. Growing up, my sister and I were always photographed together. We were often dressed in similar clothing and many people thought that we were twins. Today, we couldn't be more different.

My sister is the epitome of grace and beauty and probably what most mothers want their daughters to look like. I, on the other hand, am edgy, breaking every rule, often times hard and stern, commanding and powerful. It's clear. I defy traditionally what a woman is supposed to embody and often times behave like, through no fault of mine. I've always been this way.

But back to my story…

As we've gotten older my sister and I have shared less photographs of ourselves together for many reasons. Primarily I think it's because I allowed myself to be photographed less. I lost my confidence. The constant comparison and pressure to look like a "normal" girl, to look and act more like my sister seemed to have gotten to me at some point. I just couldn't measure up.

Most people know me as confident in my person but there were moments where I struggled with my identity. Maybe I should say that I struggled with getting people to identify me as I indentifed myself and so I dressed the way I didn't want to, so that I could appease society and oftentimes the church. When I made these compromises, there was a deep cry within myself. I felt like I was slowly killing everything that I was created to be. I wasn't being the unique personality that God created me to be.

There were so many times I heard, "You look so much like a boy," that at one point in time I wondered if something was wrong with me. I remember dedicating one year to simply looking at women to see if I'd have any sexual or physical reaction to their make up. I wanted to ascertain to myself that I really was into men and men alone.

Conclusion?

I deal in strictly men.

lifts eyes and hands to the sky

Thank you, Jesus!

Physically, I can see when a woman is beautiful but nothing inside of me leaps when I see a beautiful woman. Something certainly leaps inside of me when I see a beautiful man. I am reminded of the existence of God. And shamefully, every now and then I have a bout of lust. I think that's probably how a man feels towards a woman that he is attracted to.

So I wasn't a lesbian. I ruled that out. *deep sigh of relief*

And yes, I sighed in relief.

 At the end of the day, I am a Christian woman who believes in If I was attracted to people of the same sex, it would mean one more burden - one more cross - and one more thorn that I would have to struggle with daily. I'm happy that the burden isn't mine By virtue of being human, I already have a ton.

But I was saying...

Still, I didn't fit society's definition of traditional womanhood in my looks or actions. I prayed to God to help me be more womanly; help make my hips wider, help make them sway more when I walk. But nothing changed.

 I lie.

Some things did change. But they changed through my own doing. I tried to change who I was.

I tried to become quiet and docile and I tried to dress as they said girls were to dress. The end result was a deep-seated dissatisfaction with self and a denial of purpose. Most days, I felt like Paul; like probably this was a thorn in my side. This was the thing that I would continually have to pray about to keep me humble.

What the hell was wrong with me?

The truth is nothing was wrong with me then and nothing is wrong with me today. I simply don't fit traditional and societal constructs of womanhood. But I do fit the divine mould.

I do want to say that this letter is not me railing against tradition, culture or societal norms and values. Tradition and culture are valid. To be traditional or cultural is not to be anti-God. As a matter of fact, many anti-God movements have used defiance of societal and cultural norms to state boldly that they have chosen to go down another path.

For example, homosexuals have used and defied societal constructs such as the classification of clothing to state boldly to everyone that they are choosing to identify with an alternate gender by wearing what society deems the clothes of that gender.

Having said this, I've also seen in my own life and in the life of many that to not be traditional or cultural is not to be anti-God. In many cases, to carry the cross of going against the grain of tradition is to walk in purpose, is to bring freedom and liberation to many and it is to be who God has called one to be.

I think if I had the choice, my prayer to have the desire to behave just like every other girl would be answered and I wouldn't be writing this letter. I would be accepted. I would never have shed a tear about my ostracization and rejection in my moments of aloneness. But it has yet to go away. My prayer has yet to be answered and I've come to grips with the fact that it may NEVER be answered.

The truth is that people will probably always question my sexuality and who I am because of my personal sense of style or until I have a ring on my finger stating that some man has "claimed" me. The truth is that cultural and societal expectations of me will always render me an oddity in the sphere that is womanhood. But it is also a blatant truth that there is no justification for my womanhood except that it is divine.

I am woman because God gave me the privilege of carrying the genetic makeup that is woman. I have fallopian tubes and a womb and from my monthly encounter with menstruation ever since I was 12 I'd say they function quite well.

I often jokingly say that if I ever made the decision to engage in premarital sex that I that I would be with child with immediacy. Yes, I think myself to be that fertile. I desire the half that is the other rib and I am equipped to receive and incubate his seed. These are experiences that no man has EVER been equipped to partake of nor will they ever be able to partake of them as per divine design; as per natural design.

I will be and do things that a man cannot because I am woman. I am woman simply because I am and more importantly, I embrace it. I love being woman.

I gotta jet now or rather I'm choosing to jet now, but perhaps in a subsequent letter - or subsequent letters - I'll share with you some of the things that have been impressed on my heart about woman and the state of being woman: womanhood. Till then, I endeavor to be everything that God has designed me to be: Godly Woman.

Sincerely,
Understanding Womanhood

Dear Sister,

You may have noticed from my previous letter that the answer to the question of, "What is womanhood?" had eluded me for a long time.

Something inside me knew that the woman was equal to her counterpart found in the man. I believe that she is equal to him in rights, freedoms and the abilities that are not affected by the divine assignment of sex. Still, something inside me also aligned with the belief that we are indeed different in so many ways.

There are distinctions which have caused the classification of one human entity as man and the other as woman. But what are these distinctions?

Are these distinctions found in the sexual division of chores or labor? Is womanhood defined by the ability to cook, clean, wash, and take care of a household? Is womanhood vulnerable, in need of protection and provision? Does womanhood need to be led? Is it long, flowing hair, dresses, skirts, lipsticks and heels? What is it?

My lack of understanding about what and who I was troubled me. You see, I'm not the long-flowy-dress-wearing type of chick and there's not much I believe that I'm restricted to doing because I have a vagina. I don't cook often and I hate doing most domestic work but I'll sit in an office and work 36 hours straight.

I've always believed that with God at my side, I can conquer the world. I've always believed that I can race cars, climb trees, speak to large audiences and play musical instruments just as well as any man. I've always believed that I can pick up and travel the world all by my lonesome. I've always believed that I can build an entrepreneurial empire just as well as any man can. Still, I've always identified with being woman.
I just didn't understand its essence.

I once had dreadlocks, but today I wear my hair in a short cut and I've had men, particularly those in church, say to me that I should never have cut off my locks or that I should grow my hair out because I already possess such a masculine energy.

I've had both men and women try to bully me into compliance with cultural and societal definitions of womanhood by ascribing unto me things that I had not subscribed to; by suggesting that I was a lesbian - that I had subscribed to the movement away from the identity that God gave to me. Yet I had NEVER - and NEVER have - once in my lifetime had a desire to be with another woman. Yet I had NEVER once in my lifetime had the desire to be a man. Yet I have always identified with being woman. Yet - from my lens - I've only aspired to walk in the fullness of my womanhood.

At one point these assumptions about who and what I was hurt me, and it was largely because I didn't understand womanhood. Those who forced me into this place of hurt with their words and actions toward me unfortunately also did not understand it. My lack of comprehension as well as theirs, forced me into an unconfident space and shamefully, I sometimes tried to conform.

There were days where the simple utterance of, "I thought you were a boy" would have me reeling in confusion about what womanhood was. And if it was what they said it was then I wasn't it so what was I? I had identity issues.

Today, not so much. Today, I understand who I am. Today I understand that the perceptions of people and societal and cultural norms have nothing to do with what I was designed to be. Womanhood transcends all of these things.

Today, I understand that I am WOMAN simply because I am. I am woman because God created me as such. I am woman not because I can throw down in the kitchen like nobody's mama nor is my womanhood diminished by my lessened proclivities to other matters of domesticity. I am woman not because of the length of my hair or the vastness of my hips but I am woman because God created me as such.

I am WOMAN because God has designed me in a particular way. He has installed within me a cocktail of hormones that cause me to desire the opposite of who I am; a cocktail that causes certain reactions in response to certain feelings, a cocktail that allows my body to prepare monthly for the receipt, accommodation and incubation of a man's seed. These things are mine as per God's design, and no man can EVER naturally lay claim to them.

No man can ever say that his body is equipped to release eggs which can be fertilized by another man. No man can ever say that he experiences a period/menstrual cycle. These experiences are mine as per God's design: WOMAN. I am WOMAN for no other reason than I am.

What I've discovered about womanhood is what every woman should discover. I think it takes off the pressure. It makes it easier to learn, to grow and to better ourselves. It makes it easier for us to see ourselves as God sees us: that we are, simply because he decided that we are.

So if you've ever struggled with understanding why you are, I hope that in some way this letter has brought some measure of peace to you.

Your womanhood does not hinge on the colors you choose to wear nor does it hinge on the clothes that constitute your wardrobe. Your womanhood does not hinge on your desire or lack thereof to be married and have children nor does it hinge on your proclivity towards matters of domesticity. You are woman simply because you are.

Woman enlightened about womanhood

Dear Woman,

We've heard it so often that we've believed it. We heard it so often that we forced generations of womanhood to lose themselves; to erect barriers that purpose did not.

We've heard it so often that we've limited womanhood to the scope of becoming a man's wife and someone's mother.

Wife and mother. These are some of the beautiful experiences that come with womanhood, they are expressions of womanhood, they are exclusive to the makeup of womanhood but they are not the chief purpose of womanhood.

The chief purpose of womanhood is to reflect God in a way that manhood cannot. The existence of womanhood alongside manhood allows God to be shown in a wholeness that ceased to exist in the one human the very moment that Adam's rib was removed to form another entity.

So…

They lied when they told you that the only way that you can be of any value on this earth is by becoming a man's wife or someone's mother. They plain out lied.

They lied when they told you that your purpose is found in a man. They lied when they told you that it is God's design for you to simply become what a man desires because you were created for him. You already are, woman. You already are woman.

Before you are a man's daughter, a man's wife, someone's sister or someone's mother, you are God's child. He knew you even before you were formed in your mother's womb and formed you, he did. He placed gifts, talents and desires within you and and they were placed in you for His glory.

Don't ever let anyone tell you that you ought not to partake in certain sports or certain jobs because you are a woman. Don't ever let anyone place upon you limitations/differences that are not divine.

Play that sport, take that crazy, crazy job. Utilize all the gifts and talents that the Lord has placed within you. Do it because you're woman. Do it because it's an opportunity for you to reflect the might, power, grace, mercy and glory of The One who created you.

A sister rooting for ya.

Dear Purpose-filled Sister,

I promised you that I'd keep sharing with you some of the discoveries I've made about womanhood. I'm keeping that promise. This time, I write to you on the topic of purpose.

I believe that for a woman to live a life fulfilled - one without too many unanswered questions - she must know that her purpose is not found in a man nor is it wrapped up in becoming what any one man thinks he requires. She already is what he requires because embedded in her God-given purpose is the help which he needs. So remember, ALWAYS, your purpose comes from God.

Before Eve was brought to the man in the garden and given to him as his helpmeet she was first a reflection of the Creator's image. Therefore, like her, your first purpose is to show forth God as he is revealed in womanhood.

And no, I do not dispute that woman was made for man. No, I do not dispute that we are man's help-meet. But I dispute what they've made of it.

I dispute that this places us in a position of inferiority. I dispute that this requires us to lay aside every dream, vision and plan that the Lord has given to us for the sake of propelling the man's vision forward. Who you are - everything that you are - should propel it forward.

Again, I say God has placed within you gifts and talents. He has given you visions, dreams and plans and if marriage is ever your portion in this life, know that all of these things that he has placed in you is what will help the man fulfill his purpose. If ever marriage is your portion in this life, know and understand that everything that God has called you to be will help your husband fulfill his God-given instructions.

So I say, "Go forth. Be everything that God has called you to be. Be leaders, lawyers, teachers, doctors, engineers, contractors, masons, carpenters, athletes, millionaires and billionaires, wives, mothers, single and slaying. Be Godly women. Subdue the earth for it is your God-given mandate, woman!"

Slaying

THE TRUE MEASURE OF BEAUTY

Hey there, gorgeous.

I feel it important to let you know that you are beautiful… or is it gorgeous? Alright. Let's just go with beautiful.

You are beautiful.

You are beautiful not because of your slender frame or wide hips. You are beautiful not because of the hair which flows down your back in regal splendor nor is it because of your gorgeous fro.

You are beautiful because ye who created you deems you fearfully and wonderfully made. You are beautiful simply because you are not the product of a man but the product of an all powerful God; a God who fashioned you from the rib of an entity he spoke into being; an entity made in his own image and likeness.

When you look in the mirror you see the genesis of a protruding stomach, cellulite and stretch marks. When you look in the mirror you see scars that scream your disobedience to your parents' warnings not to climb that tree with your older brothers. I see them too.

Would it astound you to hear me say that even in light of all of these things that you remain beautiful?

I know that the brothers on the block told you otherwise. They said that your hair wasn't long enough. They said that your hips were a little too wide or that your abdominal rise was detestable. They said that you were too thin and you didn't have the derriere that would render you a sister. But they're tripping. You are fearfully and wonderfully made.

I see beauty in the way you hugged your sister when she saw the extension of her establishing alliances with another; breaking the circle which made them one. I see beauty in your loyalty and faithfulness to your family. I see beauty in the selflessness that allowed and looked forward to having another life burrowed in your center and nurtured from your breasts. All I see is beauty.

You see, I've learnt that the true measure of our beauty was NEVER to be found in the externals. It was NEVER to be found in the curve of our lips or the sway of our hips. Our beauty is about our humanity.

It is about the kind words that we speak to a broken friend. It is about the selflessness which gives our last $5 dollar note to someone whom we deem in need of it more than we do. It is about the parts which scream loudly that there is a God and woman was made in his image and likeness.

Learning Of beauty

Beautiful Sister,

They cut off a few of the things which made the woman that you are; or at least what we thought made you woman. Yet, somehow you're more woman than you've ever been. The disease weakened you yet somehow you discovered within a well spring of strength. It's aggression shook you, yet you still stand.

It robbed you of your hair, yet you still radiate with beauty; I see you clothed in grace and humility. They took away your womb and damned you to a a perpetuity of barrenness, yet you're pregnant with hope and unsurpassed strength. They cut off your breasts yet you still feed and nourish a multitude; you nourish with wisdom, strength, hope and love.

I am left to reason that the measure of your womanhood was never found in the ampleness of your breasts or in the presence of your womb, but in the weight of your soul. So when you look into the mirror, look with eyes that see into the soul and all you will see is pure, undiluted woman because that's what you are. So when you look into the mirror look with eyes that see. Look with eyes that see the fullness of the woman that you are; the woman - the reflector of God - who could NOT disappear even in the face of sickness.

Learning Of Beauty

Dear Sister,

I have seen way too much booty and boobi-es. On further ponderance, it is way more than any woman should ever see in her lifetime, and it's partly your fault.

It's your fault because you believed it when they told you that you were only worthy of attention when your skin was bared; free from the warmth or the kiss of clothes.

It's your fault because somehow you believed the lies which said that you are more beautiful and will grow in appreciative value only when you display your body in the splendor of its birth-state. Somehow you succumbed to the deception that says that you will be every man's envy if you display unclothed, RAW extensions of your self: jpeg.

The truth is that regardless of whether you do these things or not, you are beautiful. You are precious. You are valuable. And for anyone who says otherwise…

They make untruth their resting place.

Your value is not marked by your contribution to a stream of photographs dedicated to the objectification, devaluation and de-sexualization of womanhood nor is the number of likes and loves on Facebook and Instagram a true measure of your worth and womanhood.

Every time you share a picture of you in a state of undress, you contribute to the objectification of womanhood but more than that, you scream loudly that you have a limited and in some cases non-existent comprehension of your worthiness as a woman; of my worth as a woman and of our worth as women.

Know that you are worthy.

Show that you know it by sharing RAW extensions which capture soul, heart, kindness and the beauty of just being. Show that you know it. Believe it or not, you can be naked with your clothes on.

Learning Of Beauty

THE TEACHER
CALLED LIFE

Dear Miss Discontent,

Since we're on the topic of social media…

I love social media and you probably do too. We can have a "who loves social media more" contest and very few people would beat me. I'd probably win…

And I was saying: I love it. It opens us to new perspective and experience. It places us in new cultural settings right from the spots we've owned on our living room couches. But sometimes, this gift of exposure transforms into the curse of comparison.

At the risk of having you ignore every letter I write after this one, 'imma keep it real with you. As I sit typing this, I am as broke as I've ever been in my 25 years of existence. I have had $1.47 cents, not US but XCD, on my account for three months, and I think by the world's standard my net worth is somewhere around $-45,000 XCD.

I haven't purchased new clothes since my second year of university - it's almost 4 years since I left university, so you do the math - and I legit have 3 pairs of shoes: a pair of leather sandals, a pair of leather boots, and a pair of leather heels.

Hear de scene, na: If you hopped on to my social media profiles, they wouldn't quite tell these stories. Well… they kinda do. I'm wearing the same shoes and the same clothes year after year after year. So I think that my social media profiles do tell these stories. But these are not the stories that people see.

They see the story of someone who is trying. They see the story of someone determined to live every ounce of her life fulfilling purpose. And it's not because I'm keeping up appearances… maybe I am a little? Who knows? My poverty is not something I look to wear as a badge of honor. But I digress. I was saying they see what they see largely because I've chosen to be content in my space.

I say all this to say, sometimes what we see on social media is not people being fake or lying about their progress. What we see are people choosing to be content in their now and looking toward their futures with unbridled hope. We measure this displayed contentment against our discontent and at the end of the day contentment will always win.

Contentment will always look better. Contentment will always look happier. Contentment will always look richer. Contentment will always seem more accomplished. Contentment will always seem more well read. Contentment will always win.

So choose ye this moment - this day - to be content. So don't be too hard on yourself. So don't be too shaken that you haven't yet accomplished the achievement of every goal that you thought you would have already scored at 25, 30, or 35. So don't be too hard on yourself because social media tells you that other people are having an easier go of it than you are.

Many are as broke as you are. Some are worst off. Many are as confused as you are about the next step. Some have given up. And yes, some are having an easier go of it. So what? Keep your head up, girl!

Broke, But Trudging Toward Contentment

Dear Sister,

This is one of the letters that you probably wouldn't have gotten to read had this compilation gone out at the time that I had appointed for it to be out. This is one of the letters that you probably wouldn't have gotten to read had fate and time not intervened for the sole purpose of disrupting my plans. So I guess we have them to thank.

I think this letter is different in that I refuse to make the conclusions for you. You may grasp instantly an understanding of the experience that I share but there is also the possibility that you won't. My hope is that you do.

I tell a story of an always-been, super-ambitious me. I've always wanted more. I wanted to attend the best schools, wear the nicest clothes and eventually drive the nicest cars. I wanted to read the best books and own the nicest houses. I've always set the bar high and as it concerns the subject of money, I decided when I was 16 that I was going to be a millionaire.

I pursued the goal fervently for about 10 years. I was focused on one thing and one thing alone: making money. I was focused, and then I was stressed. I was focused and then I was depressed.

Because of my focus, I had failed to nurture relationships, I had failed to spend time with the people who love me, I had failed to take care of my health and I had failed to be conscious in demonstrating love, gentleness and faith.

Every morning I'd get up and wonder when I would hit the mark. Every morning I'd get up, and many times, before the gratefulness that should come with being alive had sunk into my conscious, my first thought was: How do I get closer to becoming a millionaire today? I'd be so consumed with it that I couldn't take time to simply live in the moment: sit on the beach or be grateful for all of the things that I had already accomplished.

A couple of months ago I returned home from New York. My time there had not been the smoothest and I was dead tired. I had lost the desire or the zeal to do any of the things that I had previously loved doing.

I had lost the zeal and desire to execute any of the business plans that I had written over and over for years. I was no longer as gung-ho about becoming a millionaire as I was before. All I wanted was a sense of purpose.

I had lost the desire to make my name in the field of International Politics. I had just walked the corridors of the United Nations, and it just didn't seem to fill that huge void that had made it's home in my gut. All I wanted was a sense of purpose.

I made the decision - and it was difficult - to love a little more, to spend a little more time, to worry a little less, to sit on the beach more often, to pray more often. I made the decision to give a little more of my time to my church and to my community. I made the decision to help others experience the Love of God. I made a decision to listen to more music, to write more songs, and to take more vacations with me.

I realized that it was NEVER really about the money. It was NEVER really about the prestige. For me, it was about having a sense of accomplishment; continually having something to work towards. It was about having a sense of purpose.

Right now, I'm not sure if I'll ever hit that million mark, but I can say that I am simply content to live on purpose: to make music, to write songs, to write books, to give back, and to be but a minute demonstration of the vastness that is God's glory.

Solomon said it, and I didn't understand it all these years: Everything is meaningless! While the tangibles like our work, our wealth and our toys can bring some measure of transitory fulfillment, we can never find true and lasting fulfillment outside of God.

I understand it now.

Acknowledging the Creator.

Jason graduated university at the top of his class. He double-majored in History & Economics and was particularly interested in helping create developmental prescriptions for underdeveloped regions. He knew that there was a possibility that he wouldn't get his dream job straight out of university, but two years in, he wasn't expecting to be unemployed and concerned for what he would eat every day. This was a season of trouble and he was dreading it.

Most people, like Jason, are faced with a sense of dread when they hear the word, "trouble". Trouble is not something that we embrace or want. These are hard times. These are uncomfortable times. These are times where our children are not doing well in school. These are times where we're insecure about the way we look. These are times when our loved ones die. These are times when we can't pay off our debts. These are times when everyone deserts us. These are troubling times.

But why do we so despise trouble? Is it because it is a bad thing?

A couple of weeks ago, I was doing my laundry downstairs our house. I was alone and my surroundings were quiet so I took the time as an opportunity to sit with my thoughts. I reflected on some of the difficulties that I was facing and had been facing since my exodus from university life in 2013. And I was like, "Man, I am so tired of this, God. When does this end?"

The voice of God swiftly responded to my complaints. It said, "I want you to change your perspective of trouble."

At the word "trouble", my mind's eye was given an animation of a square-headed little nuisance. He jumped from place to place, gracing any and everyone with his unwanted presence. A woman was pouring ingredients into a bowl getting ready to whisk it into a beautiful consistency and before she could finish pour in all of her eggs, he hopped unto the spoon and "troubled" the contents of the bowl. He stirred fiercely.

He jumped off the spoon and run out of the house. He was looking to impose his presence on some other unsuspecting people. As he run towards a car with a couple discussing what they were going to have for supper, he saw a puddle of water and kicked it with joy. He wouldn't be trouble if had not troubled that water. He then run towards the car with that unsuspecting couple. He shook the car with all of his might, leaving the couple startled and the car displaced.

The animation ended but by the end of that little episode where I crazily chuckled and smiled to no one or anything, my understanding of trouble had been redefined. Still, as if to cement what he was bringing to my attention, God brought to my remembrance a passage of Scripture: John 5:1-4.(NLT).

¹After this there was a feast of the Jews; and Jesus went up to Jerusalem. ²Now there is at Jerusalem by the sheep market a pool, which is called in the Hebrew tongue Bethesda, having five porches. ³In these lay a great multitude of impotent folk, of blind, halt, withered, waiting for the moving of the water. ⁴For an angel went down at a certain season into the pool, and troubled the water: whosoever then first after the troubling of the water stepped in was made whole of whatsoever disease he had.

I was familiar with the passage and the reminder added clarity to what had been provided by the animation, but I felt like I needed to read it. I rushed upstairs to my room to grab my Bible. And there it was…

At the risk of having this read or sound like a typed out sermon, turn your attention to verse 3 with me. Note the state of people before the troubled thing; in this case, water. They were impotent, blind, halt and withered. And they were anticipating a move: a move of water; a move in the water.

By this point I was near speaking in tongues. I kid. But I was bubbling with excitement. I still didn't want trouble and would take a pass on it if it was offered to me politely but I was beginning to understand it's significance.

It's significance was further heightened when God brought to my attention the significance of what was being troubled: water. I want you to think of water and its symbolism in the Bible. Water, even in secular circles is symbolic of life. Hold on to that symbolism. You'll need it.

But anyhoo…

At this point, I was like, "Ok God. I hear you. I get you. My perspective is changing. I'm definitely expecting a great move or shift in my life. I want to go from poor to rich. I want to go from proud to humble. So I'm definitely like these people at the pool waiting for a move." And then I hit verse 4.

Verse 4: Something happened; something which created the movement of water. The angel troubled the water. What? I said, the angel troubled the water. Now, remember that symbolism that you were holding onto? Let's make the conversion: The angel troubled life. The angel troubled your life.

At that point I wasn't so excited anymore. I was like, "Ok God. I hear you. This trouble that I am experiencing is here to create that movement or shift in my life that I'm desiring and asking of you". My face literally looked like a frowning smiley. But then he wasn't done. He said, "One more thing. Look at what happened after the water – your life – is troubled."

"...whosoever then first after the troubling of the water stepped in was made whole of whatsoever disease he had."

Yup. After the water was troubled and the sick embraced it for what it was, they rushed to step into it, and there was a conversion. Those who were impotent became powerful. Those who were blind gained vision, those who were halt gained movement and those who were withered became upright and alive again.

My excitement peaked again.

In applying this understanding of trouble to my life, I was encouraged to embrace troubled times. I was encouraged to see them for what they really are. I was encouraged to see them as moments that would provide clarity in my vision and fuel for my movement. I was encouraged to see them as moments that would provide a surge of power in my life; moments that would see me upright in my faith where I had withered. I learnt that there was virtue in trouble.

May be this be a lesson that you grasp too.

And my prayer for you?

The truth is that I never pray for trouble for anyone. But it is very likely that if you are human - fat, thin, wealthy, poor, bald or big-haired - you will encounter trouble. In light of this truth, I say, "Wherever there is trouble in your life, let it be fruitful."

May your troubled life thrust you into potency. May you recognize in you gifts, talents and abilities that you didn't know existed.

May your troubled life bring you into a place of vision. May you see that next business idea clearly and may you have a total grasp of the subject matter for that next book or that next hit song. May you be able to see opportunities where before you would have seen doom.

May your troubled life give you movement where you were halt. May it be the stop to your procrastination and may it foster a sense of urgency towards the accomplishment of that next goal.

May your troubled life make withered things upright and may your troubled life bring forth blessings in abundance.

For now,
Shalom!

RELEVANT
CONVERSATIONS

Dear Miss Graduate,

Today, you graduated and you didn't do it lightly. You did it with weighted GPAs, and degrees of knowledge in Economics, Law, Medicine, History, Entrepreneurship, Management, Sociology, Social Work, Physics, Computer Science and Math.

These are tremendous accomplishments and honors and I celebrate you. I applaud you. I congratulate you.

Some of our grandmothers could ONLY dream about this possibility. In some parts of the world, even today, little girls are not allowed the gift of education. But you have made this great feat. You came, you saw, and you conquered. Be proud; be happy, but also let it be about more.

Let it be about much more than the accomplishment. Let its being extend to its purpose.

Purpose in your heart to change your family, to change your community, your country and your world. Purpose in your heart that because of this feat, everything you touch, everything you impact with your words and with your life, will be BETTER.

This is more than about you being a "bad bitch". Matter of fact it has absolutely nothing to do with that. You're not an animal. This is more than about you being an independent woman. Matter of fact, it has absolutely nothing to do with that. We thrive best in our dependence on God, and in our co-operation with each other.

It is not about you.

Dare I say, don't ever make the gift of knowing about your glory or your elevation. It's a swift path to arrogance.

Instead, consider it to be you being given the tools to extend God to others. This is about you using what you've learnt to be kinder, gentler and more patient with others. It is about you using what you've learnt to make life easier and more comfortable for others. This is about you using what you've learnt to help others come closer to fulfilling their God-given purpose. In all these things, it isn't about you. Still, if you live in such a fashion it will amount to you fulfilling your God-given purpose.

Educated for Purpose

Heya sistren,

We hold to the belief that we are a combination of the 5 people that we spend most of our time with; at least I do. I believe that I become who I allow to invest in me. And for this, I subscribe whole-heartedly to the following:

Everyone deserves love and respect but everyone SHOULD not be your friend. There are some people in your circle that you need not become like. There are a few people in your circle that you need not take counsel from.

Some of them will wreck your home, your finances and your life without even recognizing it. They don't do it intentionally but they can only share with you what they know: chaos.

Some of them will suck you dry without ever giving anything in return. They don't do it intentionally but there is only so much that one can give from a place of emptiness.

Some of them will crumble the moment you need a source of strength in a difficult moment. They don't do it intentionally but many of them were taught only to lean on others; not to be a pillar of strength to others.

I say all this to say be intentional about the people you

surround yourself with.

Surround yourself with people who are encouraging and will support your successes. Surround yourself with people who won't seek to trivialize your triumphs and achievements. Surround yourself with people who won't make every success or failure of yours a competition with their success or failure. Surround yourself with people who need you but will also give back to you.

Be intentional in picking the curves which form your circle.

Intentional

Dear Weary,

Who taught you to lie so well?

One of the true testaments of strength lies in the truth of your utterances; the difficult ones; the ones which make you look weak in the eyes of others.

Strength is able to say, "No, I'm not doing so well today." Strength has the ability to say, "I fear that I'm not doing a great job of being his mother." Strength is able to say, "I am weak. I don't think I can do this alone."

It's quite normal to have moments where you feel like your world is crumbling around you. It's alright if you feel like you don't have the strength to cook or clean today. It's alright if every now and then you feel like you need a day just for you so you can recharge. It's alright.

The pressure to live up to the myth that there are some of us with perpetual S-es on our chests can be overwhelming. But don't succumb to the hype. There is no Superwoman. Then again, even if we are to believe what we read in the comic books even the Supers have a weakness: Kryptonite. We're all human. Your other sisters, like you, are just women.

I want you to know that I look to demystify the concept of the super woman not because there aren't women doing phenomenal things. I look to demystify it because super some how implies that we are without weakness.

There are days when you feel like you just can't go on and you have absolutely nothing to apologize for. In moments such as these it will take nothing away from you to call on your circle or your community for help. After all, It is in moments of weakness that you find the sources of your strength: your hubby, your friends, family, children and most importantly, your God.

Just Woman

Dear Sister,

One of my favorite quotes on the subjects of love and vulnerability comes from C. S. Lewis. He says,

"To love at all is to be vulnerable. Love anything and your heart will be wrung and possibly broken. If you want to make sure of keeping it intact you must give it to no one, not even an animal. Wrap it carefully round with hobbies and little luxuries; avoid all entanglements. Lock it up safe in the casket or coffin of your selfishness. But in that casket, safe, dark, motionless, airless, it will change. It will not be broken; it will become unbreakable, impenetrable, irredeemable. To love is to be vulnerable."

How deep is this?

Girl, it is deep. It is depth revealed in words. It is an abyss whose measurements carry one far away from society's teachings on matters of love and vulnerability.

Society teaches us how to devise mechanisms and schemes that will always carry us far from the door of hurt. This isn't necessarily a bad thing except when it is in exchange for one's ability to be vulnerable.

Society teaches that to be vulnerable is to be hurt so we live in a world where everyone is trying not to look foolish out in these streets. They're trying to accomplish these things by not being vulnerable and therefore, not loving. The thing is in the absence of love, there can only be hate.

The thing is some of us will probably settle for looking stupid for stupid things but if there is any term or condition of vulnerability attached to this stupidity, we believe that it is to be instantly rejected. But I digress. We live in a world where no one is trying to love.

I totally get it. No one wants to look stupid. No one wants to look weak. No one wants to be hurt. No one wants to be deemed less than for their display of more hope and increased faith in another. But we need love. We need to love. The world needs love.

Truth?

If we endeavor to love, if we endeavor to heal our communities and our lands, we take the risk to do just that: to be hurt, to look stupid and weak because to love is not to guarantee reciprocation. To love is to love.

When we endeavor to love, we take the risk of looking stupid out in these streets. We take the risk of loving a man who loves us and every other woman. When we endeavor to love, we take the risk of looking weak. We take the risk of having to forgive hurt so deep that it physically hurts. When we endeavor to love…

So should we not love? Should we NEVER be vulnerable?

I say love. I say love the guts out of everyone whom you encounter. And as you love, I wish for you men who will honor that love. I wish for you children who will express their gratitude in kind words, obedience, and honor. I wish for you.

And in the cases where the die of vulnerability land on the wrong side of your hope… sigh and *hugs*. I pray that you grow, that you learn, that you forgive and never lose your ability to be vulnerable; to bare your soul, to share kindness and kind words; to be an extension of God to humanity.

Learning to Be Vulnerable

Dear Frozen,

I have an obsession with doing exactly what it is that I'm supposed to do here. I often say, "I want to leave empty. I want to fulfill every ounce of purpose that I was put here to fulfill." It follows that my greatest fear is unfulfilled purpose.

I suppose to some that this is a good type of fear. I suppose to some that this fear is a worthy one. It is a fear that should exist. But it is what it is: fear. And it functions just like every other fear.

Just like every other fear, it sometimes cripples me.

I become obsessive about planning my next move. I become anxious. I become fearful that the next step I take, the next country I travel to or the next person I speak to, could be the wrong move; could be the hand that pulls the rug of destiny out from under the feet of my life and I become frozen.

But frozen people don't move. Frozen people are cold. Frozen people are lifeless. Frozen people are dead. Frozen makes me exactly what I fear: unfulfilled purpose.

I'm a little slow when it comes to these difficult lessons but I'm slowly coming to realize that for purpose to be fulfilled, life must be lived and a life lived is a life without fear.

For this reason, I've purposed to take the next flight out. I've purposed to see strange lands. I've purposed to leave unfulfilling cubicles. I've purposed to take risks. I've purposed to bring to life the seeds planted in me and I've purposed to love more. I've purposed to trust and I've purposed to care. I've purposed to say "No" to the opportunities that I do not want in the stead of grasping frantically on to everything that comes my way, fearful that I may be missing the next big thing. What's more is that I've decided to do all of these things without the fear of unfulfilled purpose simply because to fulfill purpose is to live fearlessly.

You should join me too! Let's thaw out together.

Learning to Be Fearless

DIFFICULT
CONVERSATIONS

Dear Sister,

Today, you ripped life out of you. Those who've gone before you tell me that it is something that you'll forever carry yet it is a part of you perpetually lost. I can't imagine the pain nor can I imagine the thoughts which accompany you on this part of the journey.

Truth?

I don't know what to say.

I've learnt that sometimes even beautifully strung sentences are inadequate to soothe the sting of the measure of pain that we'll experience on this earth. I've learnt that sometimes they are downright useless.

So this letter isn't so much about me talking as it is about me saying that I love you. I don't judge you. I don't know why you did what you did. Even in the midst of what I think to be a self-inflicted pain, I hurt for you.

What's more I have a friend that I think you should talk to. He loves you even more than I do and his love comes with no conditions attached. He is waiting for you with arms open wide.

He'll forgive you the things that you can't forgive yourself. He'll love you when you don't feel like you deserve to be loved.

Truth?

I don't know if the pain will ever go away. I don't know that you'll ever be at peace with you. But I do know that in His arms you can find some measure of consolation; consolation better than what I can give through words on a page.

So for now, I put my pen down and I give to you the consolation of my silence.

Your Sister.

A few years ago, I attended a Christian camp as a camp counselor. Most Christian camps have a session on sex and sexuality where young men and women are taught what God expects where sex and sexuality are concerned and this camp was no different.

At this particular camp the young men and women were separated for this session; not for the purpose of keeping matters veiled but for the purpose of encouraging a level of openness which perhaps would not have happened if both sexes were in the same room at the same time. That day changed my life. I became aware that I formed part of a minority and it wasn't because of the color of my skin; it was because I had never been sexually molested as a child.

Campers and camp counselors alike had experienced one or more than one traumatic experience where a family member, a friend, or someone in authority whom they trusted had violated their trust and defied their duties to protect that child. My sister, my cousin and myself were stunned to say the least, and then the tears came down. I couldn't contain it. I couldn't believe it.

Dear Sister,

You shared with me that you are part of the majority, and my disbelief was multiplied. I convey to you my deepest apologies. I want you to know that despite the voices in your head, there was nothing you did to deserve this. It had nothing to do with the way you were dressed. It had nothing to do with your beautiful smile. It had nothing to do with your early growth spurt.I don't care if you stripped naked and run around the house, he, she, they had no right to.

This has everything to do with your abuser's lack of integrity. They are men and women who were entrusted with the duty of guiding you along life's path yet violated that duty in the most despicable of ways. This has everything to do with men and who cannot be trusted not to violate or abuse the sacredness of responsibility. This has everything to do with your older cousin's lack of restraint and sometimes it has everything to do with hurt people hurting others. But believe me, it has absolutely nothing to do with you.

I know that you have been hurt in unmentionable ways. I know that you sometimes find it difficult to define for yourself an identity untainted by the dirt of the violation you endured. I know that many have judged you harshly without being privy to the pain and confusion that you carry inside. I know that you have unanswered questions and seemingly incurable wounds. I may never be able to fully understand what this has done to you but I believe unwaveringly - fully - that you can overcome.

My belief is not an "I'm sorry that you experienced this but stop using this as an excuse for your bad behavior" type of belief. My belief is not an "I'm sorry that you went through this but it's time for you to get over this" type of belief. My belief is an "If you're still standing here today after this gross violation of your humanity, you can overcome anything." type of belief.

I believe unwaveringly that you can stand firm in God's design for you; that you can turn away from the definition that abuse sought to give to you. I believe that you can dispose of all of the hurt and pain which has planted itself in your heart and in your gut for so many years. I believe that you can heal. I believe that you can recover.

Maybe you don't believe. But I believe for you.

Don't ask me why. I probably wouldn't be able to answer. But I believe for you.

Perhaps its because my stated beliefs are my prayers for you, and perhaps it is because I believe that our prayers are only made effective by our belief in their plausibility. So even as you roll your eyes, shake your head and the tears stream down your face - even as your thoughts say that this is something that you'll always carry with you and that "she'll" never understand - I'll keep believing simply because I pray for you wholeness in your spiritual identity, your physical identity, your emotional identity and your sexual identity.

Heartfelt Prayers

To My Sister With Identity Issues,

I've started penning this letter several times. I've also stopped several times. Your plight is one difficult to address. Your plight is one that makes me uncomfortable.

Perhaps I'm uncomfortable because I see how I could have very well become you. Perhaps I'm uncomfortable because I know the backlash that could ensue when I share my views on the subject. The truth is I understand that there are few things more painful than for one to not understand who one is. I don't particularly like dealing with painful things.

Those whose understanding of themselves align with societal and cultural understandings of who and what they should be never quite understand why others who are not as lucky as they, search so relentlessly for an answer to the question of "Who am I?".

Those whose understanding of themselves mesh with societal and cultural constructs of what they should be very rarely seem to understand that not knowing who you are strikes the very center of your existence: your purpose; your reason for being.

In setting the stage for what I'm about to say, I should probably let you know that my stance is one predicated on my faith. In setting the stage for this letter, I'd like to say that you may not necessarily like every perspective that I hold on the subject. In setting the stage for this letter, I'd like to say that though my views may differ that I'll never be callous because I understand your dilemma.

Though I understand it and I would love nothing more than to relieve you of your pain and your confusion by saying the words that would bring some measure of comfort to you, I probably can't. I can't say, "Live your truth". I can't say, "You were born that way so be you." I can't offer you any of the platitudes that would render you comfortable in your state of confusion.

I begrudge you these platitudes because I wish for you to live and experience God's heart for you; God's best for you.

I begrudge you these platitudes because I believe that a decision to live contrary to what God has created you to be is a decision to settle for less than God's best. I begrudge you these platitudes because I trust God's wisdom, His design and purpose for you.

He called you woman and though I believe that womanhood is not what we have reduced it to, I also believe that it comes with a distinct God-given, God-designed sexual identity. I believe that the woman was made for the man. I believe that God designed us male and female, in his image. I also believe that when it comes to sexuality, the fullness of God's glory can only be reflected in a sexual union between a man and a woman.

I do not wish for you to feel broken or beaten. I do not wish for you to feel ostracized or unwanted. This is me simply saying that I want God's best for you.

The conclusion of this letter should probably begin now. But as I read over the words that I've written, I question why I was even reluctant to address your plight in the first place.

As my thoughts wander, I realize that the issue with identity is something that every human being can identify with; an issue that every human has experienced. And perhaps if we seek not to separate issues of sexual identity from the issues we experience in the other realms of identity - emotional, physical and spiritual - then we can remove the contrived complexities surrounding the issues of sexual identity; that you can better hear us in the stead of feeling beaten by us.

I think if we can see that the issue with identity emerges anytime we seek to live out of God's best for us, then we can recognize that the issue with identity is something that the liar, the glutton, the reveler, the fornicator, the alcoholic, the drug addict, the narcissist, the thief, the boaster - as well as the homosexual, bi-sexual and transsexual - can identify with.

For all the times that we've made you feel like your wrongs were so much greater; for all the times we've made you feel like there is no redemption for your inability to understand who you are, I apologize. But I must end for now, and I end with this.

Ultimately, God's heart is for us all to live in satisfaction - happily - with the way that he has created us; fulfilling that which he formed us for. For this, I pray that wherever you experience a tug of war with identity, that you will seek out God's heart for you and aspire to it.

Wanting God's Best For Ya

Dear Sister,

Please. Please. I beg of you: Please walk away from the bottle of death which sits on your night stand. Please shut out the encouraging chorus in your head and please choose not to hear the symphony which is intent on creating the mood ripe for your departure from this earth.

Everything - the actions of everyone - seems to be saying that your presence here is no longer necessary or wanted but I promise you that these are nothing but lies. You are loved, you are appreciated and simply because you were born you are a vessel of great purpose. Do not abort purpose. Do not switch off the light that you are.

I know that it feels like no one understands. I know that we cannot for a moment fathom the hurt and the pain that strike the very core of your soul. But even in the midst of these obstacles it is sure that you have great purpose.

If you're reading this letter, perhaps it is a message from the Most High. Perhaps this is exactly what you need to hear. Perhaps this is what you need to read to remind you that there are people who would be willing to take a phone call from you. Perhaps this is what you need to read to prompt you to visit the office of a therapist or a counsellor. Perhaps this is what you need to shoot a random stranger an email and say that you need help (I'm available at chadia@wakonte. com). I pray that this what you need to heed my cries of, "Please. Please. Please walk away from the invitation to your premature death."

Praying for Ya.

SINGLE & SATISFIED

Dear Christian and Single,

You sent me this letter and I died of laughter; mostly because I see myself in you; mostly because I've been pondering on the same things and mostly because I'm aspiring to change them.

Many young women in church who want to be married will remain single because we have perpetuated that men ought to "lead" them. So my sister with her Super Saiyan Spirituality be turning down God fearing men because they're not quite where she is yet for no other reason than, "he is not ready to lead me". *shudders of incomprehension* I used to say that nonsense too. Your girl been delivered. Thank you, Jesus!

Young lady, if he is God fearing and it is evident in his fruits then you need no more. The truth is that the Christian walk is no straight path. Our journeys are different. It is quite possible for you to enter a period of wilderness when your husband's walk is like trees planted by a river and vice versa. It is in these instances that we find the beauty in aspiring to oneness in Christ. Stap it!

Many young women in church who want to be married will remain single because we have perpetuated that men ought to "lead" them. So my sister with her 6-figure salary be turning down God fearing men who are making 5-figure salaries for no other reason than, "he is not ready to lead me because he won't be the breadwinner of our home". *shudders of incomprehension* I used to say that nonsense too and I still say it because maybe in juxtaposition to all of the assumed depth that I hold, I'm a tad bit shallow. I need deliverance!

Young lady, you are called helpmeet. Your job is to be his support, his strength and his protection. Everything that you have been called to be by God will help him be everything that he has been called to be.

Sometimes who you are is the wife who makes more money than her husband and it is quite fine for your Christian husband to be making less money than you. If he is not lazy, and concerned about your well-being and the little people that you all brought to earth, your house will run fine. You and your children will see him as the human being that he is and still treat him with honor and respect. It is in these instances that we find the beauty in aspiring to oneness in Christ. Stap it!

Then again, you don't have to stop it. But just so you know, this is #whyyoureChristianandsingle; at least that's why I think you are.

There are also the reasons that you have no control over. I think at the heart of the matter is the truth that marriage is not a guarantee for everyone. It is not a promise for everyone. There is no covenant from above that says that everyone who has a desire to be married will be married. Taking these things into consideration, I think the best way forward is to find yourself in a state of satisfaction in your singleness. This is not at all neglecting to be hopeful that the Lord has fashioned someone specifically for you. But hey, if he doesn't… Be content with you and Jesus.

Single & Satisfied

Dear I Want Marriage and Babies,

I meet so many women like you who are not content with their lives. For the life of me, I can't figure out why. Why, girl?!!

You all have loving families and great friendships. You all have amazing careers which allow for amazing experiences through helping and empowering others. You all enjoy travel and exploration. You all enjoy food and wine from distant lands. You have God in your hearts and in your homes. So why aren't you content and happy?

Because you lack marriage and babies?

I think marriage to be a beautiful institution; an institution divine in its makeup. I think the same thing of motherhood. It can only be a God thing to be given the privilege of life nestled in your womb, to birth it and to nurture it. But I also believe that before we teach any little girl how to be a wife or how to be a great mother that we must first teach her to be successfully single.

Singleness is the most natural and only guaranteed state for our human existence. It is therefore complete. It is therefore no different from marriage in being a "God thing." And we've somehow missed that.

Because we've missed it, in their every waking and growing moment we've taught little girls to be wives and mothers. We've trained them and given them the tools to walk this journey extended, ONLY for the accommodation of the needs and wants of a husband and children. We've trained them to see their purposes ONLY in wifehood and motherhood and and in doing so we've triggered the thought process that to be single is to lack.

We've done our little girls - our women - an injustice of the highest order.

To teach our little girls and women to be successfully single is not to take them away from preparation for marriage. To teach them to be successfully single is to prepare them for every facet of life: singleness, marriage, and sadly, divorce, and widowhood.

You see to be successfully single means to live a life extended; extended not just to a husband and children, but extended to humanity as a whole.

To be successfully single means to find contentment in being kind to the homeless man on the street, in clipping your grandmother's toenails, in calling in to see if your parents are alright, in reaching out to someone who is hurting, in being curled up on your couch with a good book, and in being able to grow your love for people from divers cultures and walks. To be successfully single is to walk well in your first and prime purpose: to reflect God's glory.

I think if we teach these things then more of our girls will grasp an understanding of purpose. I think if we teach these things that we'd have more content women on this earth: single and married. I think if we teach these things then some of my sisters will not feel the sting of failure that often accompanies the inexperience of the joys of marriage. I think if we teach these things more of my sisters would see marriage purposefully as opposed to seeing it as an aid for their completion. I think if we teach these things…

Love,
Single and Satisfied

ASPIRING TO ONENESS

Dear Sister,

I was cleaning up my inbox on Facebook the other day and I saw a particular message. A few months ago a young lady sent me a message asking, "How do you go about doing this dating thing as a Christian?"

At the time I was preparing to travel and I had a lot on my plate so I told her to I'd get back to her. But even when I was less busy and I contemplated the question, I realized that I didn't have an answer for her, and it's probably because I've never done the dating scene and I probably never will.

Don't get me wrong. There's nothing wrong with the dating scene. It's just not my thing. And it's not my thing probably because I cannot give my heart to a man who I'm not first friends with.

My definition of romance is intimacy. It's about the long conversations that give me a glimpse of you as a child and what our children will possibly behave like. It's about burgers and fries and trash talking over NBA games. It's about the moments that say that I don't want to be anywhere else but on this couch.

But I digress. So it's a few months later and I still don't have an answer for the young lady because hell, I've been single for 26 years of my life. But I will say this:

1.   There is a book that you need to stay in.

2.   Stay in this book. Love it. Study it. Live it. Share it. Share Love. Become a reflection of its source.

3.   Entertain a man who loves this book and spends time with it. Why? Because it is only by spending time in this book that he will know God and thus be able to identify the God in you. If he sees Him in you, he will run to you, and pursue you without fear.

You see, I've gathered from the Creation account that the very essence of man draws him to God. This is what he was created for. When he hears Him or sees Him, he runs toward communion with Him - except in his downfall - except when he becomes a marred version of what he was created to be.

So please, do not sweat the brothers. If marriage is to be your portion this life, be your best reflection of God and a man who is rooted in him will definitely run toward you.

P.S. That Book is the Bible

Chadia

Dear Sister,

Today marks two months before we celebrate your union. I am happy for you. I rejoice with you.

You are about to embark on a journey as beautiful as it is difficult; as worthy as it is painful. And hell, I'm looking forward to cutting up a rug in celebration with you.

You've probably already done your pre-marital counseling sessions. Girl, please do not skip that part of it. At all. But hey, whether you've done it or not, it doesn't hurt to make sure that you are walking down the aisle for the right reasons because hear me when I say, "Marriage, does not a broken relationship fix."

Marriage is not atonement for your guilt.

It is a beautiful union between two people who are ready to commit to being expressions of Christ to each other. If you feel wretched about all the premarital sex that you've engaged in, marriage won't fix that. That is an issue to be dealt with you and your Maker. Pray about it. Understand that you transgressed but that you're forgiven.

Marriage does not magically produce ambition or financial

management skills.

If your credit is bad, the issue is that you probably can't manage your finances or your appetites. You may need to take a class, or two, or three… You may need to learn to practice some self control.

If he's lazy, marriage won't automatically render him industrious.

Marriage does not make people work towards oneness nor does it engender commitment. Instead, it requires two people who want to work to oneness.

Please, I beg,. Do not marry this man hoping that he'll be on the same page as you are because of a ring. If he can't find the time to spend with you, and his boys are his priority, it's very very likely that you'll only get a married version of his dysfunction. Be good with who he is today.

Marriage is not a lust manager.

It is very likely that if you or he cannot contain yourselves before marriage that you won't be able to do the same within the bounds of marriage. He won't stop cricking his neck every time a beautiful woman passes by simply because he's now wearing a ring on his left finger. It just won't happen.

If you've considered all of these things and you think you're good to go. Let's make it happen! Lehwe celebrate!

Love ya!

Dear Sister,

Before I even say anything, I must put in a disclaimer: I am as single as a dollar bill. I don't want you thinking that I met the one and that you have a wedding to attend anytime soon; at least not mine.

Why are you scrounging up your face?

My apologies for your deflated excitement. Girl, I am 25, broke and busy and YOU know that I'm not entering any relationship with these labels attached to my name.

Anyhoo, I met this beautiful man. Beautiful, inside and out! He is a really cool dude - humble, doesn't talk much, quick to give these gentle answers that turn away wrath and he has a growing desire for the things of God. Now on paper, the dude is cool. Real cool. Even though I knew he was cool I said to myself, "Chadia, you could never date this dude." He was a good dude, yet I wasn't interested.

Knowing whose affections and pursuits to say yes to is no easy feat. Some of us have some how duped ourselves into believing that we have the monopoly on the idea of what a good man is. Some of us believe that if a string of men are placed before us that we'll know with all definitiveness who to pick based on our preferences and abhorrences. I've come to recognize that if I pick on my own that I am almost guaranteed to fail.

Truth be told, there are some elements that I am attracted to which definitely do not make for a good mate or a good relationship. I've learnt to allow the God who lives within me to pick. He has the monopoly on the idea of what a good man is. Not only did he create man with an idea of what his perfection ought to be but I know that he always desires what is best for me; best for you; best for us.

Trust Him.

Trust Him when he says that humility is to be desired in comparison to the swagger and cockiness that so often meets your mark.

Trust Him when he says that integrity and ambition is to be desired over a fat wallet which gained its girth by any means necessary.

Trust Him when he says that a man who can tell you that you're wrong in love is better than one who will woo you with flattery.

Trust Him.

Dear Author,

If you tell me one more time 'bout what Heather and Cornelius did while they were courting, engaged or 'bout what they do in their marriage… *cuts eyes*

I have the utmost respect for Heather and Cornelius Lindsey. But believe me when I say that your relationship, courtship or marriage is definitely not about mimicking theirs.

When Heather Lindsey shared with young men and women all across the world the story of the particulars of how God prepared her for, and how she met her husband, I do not believe that she was saying that this is exactly how you must meet your man, this is exactly how God will speak to you concerning your husband, and these are the specific things that a man MUST do in order for you to consider him your husband.

I think she shared her story to show how God worked in her life. I think she shared her story to elucidate on the importance of purity and contentment in Christ. I think she shared her story to show how God gave her the desires of her heart because she delighted in Him. I think she shared her story to encourage young men and women to pursue and submit to those of character and substance.

But many have taken this story and run with the particulars. Many have adopted Heather and Cornelius's blue print and have sought to become imitations of them. Many have rejected good men and women simply because they did not fit the exact mould that was Heather or the exact mould that was Cornelius.

When I read the Bible, I see many love stories, some with similarities and some so shocking that I find it hard to believe that God had a hand in these things.

In Sarah and Abraham's love story, I see the love story of a man who was so enamored with his wife that he lied to protect the sanctity of the union that was theirs. In this same love story, I see a man who was so enamored with his wife that he heeded from her directions that were not in keeping with what God had spoken to them about their destinies.

In Ruth and Boaz's love story, I see the story of a widowed woman who found love again in a circumstance that I pray daily that I am not asked to replicate. She pursued a man at God's bidding. In a direct translation from Saint Lucian Kwéyòl, "she brought herself to the man".

In Hosea, I see the story of a man who was called to do the seemingly impossible. It was one of the most heart-wrenching, yet one of the most profound love stories shared in the Bible; only second to that of Christ and the church.

Hosea was called by God to marry a woman who was "ratchet" and "loose". She was a prostitute who left her husband several times, committed adultery with several men, even "give d man boatwin", yet each time he went back for her and upon her return treated her no less than his bride.

Looking at this array of stories I wonder why then we have been made to believe and have believed that all of our stories ought to conform to a certain set of particulars? Why then are we passing off cultural norms and values as Biblical precedent? Why then are we making other people's preferences our own?

I have learnt that beyond the kisses and hugs, marriage ought to be an embodiment of the love that Christ has for his church; of her love toward him. I've learnt that marriage is more than matching outfits and family portraits. It is an institution that allows us to fulfill God's purpose for our lives. What God may seek for you to learn from marriage is not what he may seek for another to learn from marriage.

So relationship goals?

Christ and His Church. God's will for you.

And I leave you with this:

Ultimately, some of us will be called to love characters who are more troublesome than others while some of us may be called to love paragons of virtue. But I can guarantee you this much: our love stories do not have to be, and will not all be the same.

Writing My Own Story

DEALING
WITH OUR
BROTHERS

Dear Sisters,

Our brothers are broken and fragile too.

We so often expect them to be strong. We so often expect them to be everything that we need that we often overlook the fact that so many of them have been shattered.

We often overlook the fact that so many of them are easily shatter-able by our words and expectations. As their sisters, their mothers, their future wives, let us play our roles in restoring them, in aiding their journeys to completion as opposed to using them for our completion. For these things to be fulfilled we must first understand that our desire for the man is not to be for our completion but our extension and expansion as human beings..

So yes. I done chat in this letter. In the words of a dear friend, "Carry on nicely."

Chadia

Dear Sister,

The true mark of love leaves no stain on your skin.

If he must use your body as a canvas for his presentation of hues of black and blue then he is simply an artist who seeks to damage something already beautiful: you.

If he must break your bones or your teeth as a display of his pottery then he is an artist who does not understand that you were created beautifully and masterfully and that his attempts to "love" you only mar you.

Your body was never meant to be broken, beaten and bruised. The original painter meant only for it to be made alive through gentle strokes and soft hues.

The full expression of who you are was never meant to be subdued. You are a reflection of a powerful God's glory.

You were not created to be battered into silence; it'll only bring death. That mouth was created to speak life, kiss life, give life.

My sister, before I tell you bounce you must know and understand that you were never meant to be abused. True you are a vessel fit for use, but trust me when I say that you were never meant to be abnormally used.

Digest that. Internalize it. Believe it. Now, bounce!

Chadia

Dear Sister,.

You've somehow deceived yourself into believing that you can make him stay; that maybe if you do and allow certain things that you can keep him.

You permit him the craziest things.

You give him passes to cheat. You tell him that it is alright to go to the strip club to touch the body of a woman who is not you as long as he clears it with you before.

You allow him entry to your body when you know that he has just shared the same gift of passion with another.

You tell him that you will endure ounces of disrespect as long as it doesn't measure up to a pound.

How much more of yourself will you compromise for the sake of keeping him? How much more of yourself will you give to keep his version of love persistent?

Perhaps the questions above are enough to help you see what I'm getting at. But just in case they weren't, I'll attempt to state it plainly:

The things that you do should NEVER be seen as deposits on the account of "Keeping Him". The things that you do are about your choice to love him. They are about how you choose to demonstrate your love for him.

If he wants to step because you will not stand for disrespect, then let him step. If he wants to go, because your response to disrespect is, "Hell, No" then let him go.

Hear me when I say that you are worth so much more than conditional love. You are worth the promise of a lifetime without your heart, your acts and the essence of who you are held ransom. Free yourself from the bonds of mental, emotional - and dare I go as far as saying - spiritual kidnap.

If in the presence of his version of love the fullness of you does not appear then he MUST disappear for he is the vessel that carries that which is as the ink which taints the purity of His Love.

Chadia

Heya girl,

The wise man said, "Out of the abundance of the heart the mouth speaketh". I don't think truer words have ever been spoken. If you really want to know what people think of you, listen.

I watched him and then I heard him. I saw the anger which contorted his face, and I watched the fire of rage which burned in his eyes. Then he said it, "You stupid bitch!"

I heard him call you a bitch; a stupid one at that. I saw that everything in him sought to hurt you.

Three simple words, "You stupid bitch!" declared loudly what this man thinks of you.

Today, you tell me that you all have reconciled. Today, you tell me that he brought you flowers and that he said the he did NOT mean a word of what he said.

Here's what I believe: If someone says something to you, they damn well mean it.

If he calls you, "slut, bitch, hoe or gold digger" in the heat of an argument, this is exactly how he sees you. He views you derogatorily and as beneath him and so it is his intention to hurt you by demeaning you.

If he often tells you that you can do nothing right. He means it. He sees you as nothing but incompetent.

The mouth always reveals what is in the heart.

Who says something they don't mean?

Still, I'm not telling you to leave your man right this moment. Still, I'm not telling you to divorce your husband. I'm not saying desert him because he doesn't understand that his mouth is the spout for the substance of his heart. I'm really not telling you to do anything. That ball is in your court.

I am, however, saying that he means what he says. I am, however, saying that something about his heart towards you needs to change. I am saying that the substance of his heart towards you is not a thing of beauty. I am saying that the reflection of his heart towards you is not one that esteems you. His mouth revealed the contents of his heart.

On second thought…

Girl, Run!

Dear Sister,

It's alright to talk a great game about what you require of a man. You expect him to have a job, a car, a down payment on his first house and you would love it if he has no kids. Some people think that you're high maintenance but these are simply your standards and there's nothing wrong with having them. In the same token, I encourage you to extend similar standards to yourself.

I think it unfair that we expect these things from our brothers yet fail to meet similar expectations. Do you also have a job, a car, or a down payment on your first house?

And hey, I'm not knocking your old school values. If you'd like your man to have these things in the the name of traditionalism, are you prepared to cook, to clean and to do his laundry or do you think that your beat face, well placed hair and fit body is value enough?

I say all this to encourage you to bring something of value to the table called "relationship". Bring intellect, bring great conversation, bring support, bring encouragement, bring maturity and sensibility.

All of us, men and women, are works in progress so while you may not have it all together right now, be sure that you are at least getting it together. The term is so frequently misused that I hesitate to use it to capture what I wish to say. Still, I say,: be a WOMAN OF VIRTUE.

Love,
Chadia

Dear Sister,

I'm learning that I'm probably not the most committed person in the world. Or is it that I'm very slow to commit to anything? I don't know when it happened but it did. I'm just not as committed as I used to be.

I will leave something alone if I feel like it's not breeding the results that I expect it to breed in the time that I expect it to. I will cut someone off if I feel like they're wasting my time and energy.

But I've stayed true to my companies.

I am committed to my companies. In bad times and in good times I've stuck with them. I've wanted to leave them and call it a day, but I stayed.

Every time I think of the thousands of dollars I've invested, the late nights and the early mornings, the persecution, the ridicule and lack of support, I buck up and I get right back to it. This is not something that I can leave behind. It must work. The distinctions between my commitment to my companies and my commitment to some people, things and projects made me realize something. I realize that people are committed to what they value and they value what they've invested in.

Girl, if he's not investing in you, then he won't commit. If he's only taking from you - if he's only draining your energy and your finances without giving anything in return - then he's very very likely not committed to you. If he NEVER calls or texts, or makes any effort toward your relationship then he's probably not committed. If you're the ONLY one investing time and energy then it is likely that you're the only one committed.

And do not for a moment think that this letter is just about a gauge of his commitment toward you. This is also a good time to decide if you're committed to him.

If you're wasting this man's time, ignoring his calls and suggestions for dates then you're just not committed.

If you're only concerned for what he can buy you: a diamond necklace, a ring or a new car, then you're not committed. If you don't take time to build this man with your words in the stead of tearing him down then you're probably not committed.

Stop wasting the brother's time. Stop using him for what he can buy you. Stop using him to buffer questions about when you're going to get married or make babies. If you're not serious about the brother, let him go.

A Commitment Phobe

Hey girl,

Our parents had to do less of this than we did: of that I'm sure. We are part of a generation of men and women who live in a society that dictates that it is absolutely lawless to have a best friend with the same private part as you do. Your best friend MUST be someone of the opposite sex.

Now, I'm not bashing opposite sex best friends because it is highly likely that if I am forced to state the name of a best friend the name would most likely belong to someone of the opposite sex.

I love my male friends. You will most likely find me in the company of someone who is male and more often than not that male friend will be single.

As I get older, I'm finding that the level of closeness that I share with my male friends has decreased significantly and I'll share with you why.

My male friends are finding themselves in relationships with women who aren't me and I automatically find myself doing something of great importance when they do.

It really started to hit home for me when one of my best

liming buddies found himself in a relationship.

One time the guy and I planned to eat and go catch a movie together an entire week before the date. As a matter of fact, he was the one who lamented that we had not hung out in some time so we should catch up. But before we headed to the movies I needed to make a short stop to pick up some girl stuff at a particular store. So we ducked in, I picked up the stuff and I'm about to pay for my items.

Ring ring

"Hey babe."

I'm looking into a far off land because the conversation really has not a thing to do with me but I'm certainly not expecting what's about to come.

"Chadia, I gotta go to Timbuktu. Jasmine needs me to come do the groceries with her."

And I am serious as a heart attack. Well he didn't have to go to Timbuktu (it was a bit of a distance from where we were) but he did leave to go and help his girl do the groceries on his PA I I (no ride which is quite common for someone within our age bracket in the Caribbean region).

You can imagine that I'm upset. I'm upset not because he ditched me. But I'm upset because I'm an introvert who needs to gather up a tremendous amount of energy to leave my house and I had just done that. I'm upset because an hour before I had turned down FREE food to hang with him. I am very very upset because I now have to tread back to a house with only CRIX in my cupboard when I was just offered AMAZING free food.

Does anyone understand my dilemma?

Anyways, when I was done being pissed, and called my sister to laugh at what had just happened, I sat on my bed and spoke to myself because that's just what normal people do. I said to my self, "Chadia, he has an obligation to the woman that he committed to. You are not his woman. What he did was perfectly fine (Not… after I had cleared my day). " But seeing that he did not see it fit, I would NEVER tell the young man to tell his girlfriend, "Babe, I had plans with Chadia for a week prior and since this isn't an emergency, would it be alright if I came after?"

Now some of you are saying, "Girl, the man should have told his girl that he had plans. This isn't an emergency."

And I'm saying, "Some of y'all be tripping." Hahaha.

LETTERS TO MY SISTER

99

This what our generation doesn't understand: Redefining Relationships (this is also the thing I automatically do).

When I speak of redefining relationships, I speak of change. It requires one to examine the terms and conditions of a particular relationship and to make the changes necessary where interaction and commitment are concerned. This is for the sake of guarding one's heart as well as for the sake of the guardianship of other hearts.

I know that some of you all don't want to hear this, but I must say it: Redefining relationships are important when your friends of the opposite sex enter into committed relationships or make a commitment in marriage to men and women who are not you. This has always been a personal rule of mine and it has only served me well. More often than not, friendships fill some need/void in our lives. In as much as we don't wish to admit it, the truth is that when two single people of the opposite sex share, interact and spend quality time there is always the potential for more to happen. I think I can only pick about 4 of my many male friends for which there is absolutely NO potential. Even then, I can't say 0%.

Now this may not apply to ALL your friends of the opposite sex, but if you take some time to examine why you are friends with the men that you're friends with you'll begin to see the bits that fall into the category of potential: similar sense of humor, similar stance on faith, similar hobbies and interests, etc.

Are you crazy? I was here first.

Yes you were. But please allow me to burst your bubble.

The moment that your friend decided to commence a relationship with someone who isn't you, that friend inadvertently decided that someone who isn't you should take first priority and he relegated you to a secondary priority. I am not saying that this friend no longer cares about you. I'm simply saying that he– as he should – has reorganized the roles of various people (including yours) in their lives, and you should be happy to accommodate and encourage that shift, change or redefinition.

Where did you get this hogwash from?

Hey, my principle has Biblical foundations.

In accordance with Biblical principle, when a man becomes married, it is a divine expectation that there is to be a reorganization of roles/redefinition of roles with his parents – the most prominent and first relationship in his life. He is expected to leave his parents and cleave to his spouse. The same can be applied to other relationships.

He is also going to have to leave some friends in the name of cleaving. And sometimes when he can't do it – if you happen to be the friend that needs to be left – for his sake and his spouse's sake, it will come down to you to do the right thing: Redefine.

Someone Who's Mastered the Art of Re-defining

Dear Sister,

I read something and I think it's absolute nonsense. Mwe fache!

Boys: *Let's chill*

Men: *When are you available this week? I'd like to take you to dinner.*

'Imma just keep it real. Y'all need to stop listening to these women who are already married with a warm pair of thighs in their beds. They tryna' keep y'all from enjoying the same thing.

Why can't we allow everyone to have their personalities?

There are men who will ask you out by saying, "When are you available this week? I'd like to take you to dinner," whose only intention is to sex you after dinner and there are "boys" who will ask you out by saying, "Let's chill" and treat you with great respect.

Sister, let your picker be the Holy Spirit. Let your picker be your observation of him when he doesn't know that you are looking. But please do not decide if a man is worthy of your time by deciding what his intentions are because his preferred style of communication is not "refined".

Sister girl, refinement does not equate respectful; well maybe it does to a certain extent…

Don't get me wrong. I'm not asking you to make apologies if you prefer a man with a more refined approach. However, please do not make another man feel like he is less than if his approach lacks the air of refinement that you seek.

ALWAYS make it known that disrespect is unacceptable but NEVER make it so that unrefined ALWAYS equates disrespect. Because hell… It doesn't.

Keeping It Real

DEALING WITH OUR SISTERS

Hey girl,

Today I saw something absolutely baffling. I saw two of our sisters physically fighting over the claim to ONE brother.

Today, I saw something that escaped my realm of comprehension. I heard one of our sisters call another one of our sisters a "BITCH" and told her that if she didn't stay away from her man that she would do to her something which registered heavily on the scale of violence.

It always amazes me to see women band against each other when men have violated and disrespected them. Why do we feel that it is important to castigate, and violate another version of us when our husbands, or boyfriends are the ones who have violated us?

Why did she choose to castigate another; one who didn't make a commitment to her in marriage? Why did she argue with a woman who did not stand in front of her friends, family, church and God to say that she would be faithful to her, that she would love, honor and cherish her, and be with her for better or for worst?

I believe that some of us have sold ourselves short. We've not been cultured to believe that it is alright to hold a man accountable for his wrong actions toward us. We have not understood that it is alright to point out to our husbands or our significant others that they have failed in their commitments toward us. Instead, we attack the one who is just like us. We attack the other woman.

Sister girl, I don't think that addressing the "jabal" should ever be a part of the solution to your problem; that is, unless your address to her is an invitation to the love of God. I don't think that you should EVER think of speaking to her in antagonism. She does not have a responsibility to uphold your marital vows. But HE does.

You are telling her to leave your man alone?

Isn't this the same man who brought another entity into the circle that was designed with space only for the two of you?

Sister, believe me when I say that he doesn't need your help to tell her what's up.

He doesn't need your help to tell her that he wants to take the necessary steps to mend his breaking marriage and that he is no longer going to entertain her. He didn't need your help bringing her in, and he doesn't need it getting her out. If you are going to "act a fool" to tell this other woman to "leave your man alone" then just let him handle it, because he REALLY doesn't need your help.

Tell Him… That He is Wrong!

Hey Human That is Woman,

A few days ago I went out. It's a rare thing. Perhaps I don't go out enough. Perhaps my lack of social exposure was responsible for the shock that I felt when I saw two sisters who loved the presence of one another greet each other with, "Hey, bitch".

I can only come to one conclusion: Some of us have taken our appreciation for the talents of Dr. Doolittle just a little too far.

When did it become right to refer to another human being as a bitch, a heifer, a pig or a dog?

When did it become acceptable for us to call ourselves bad bitches and revel in "bitchery"?

Why do we dutifully and proudly confer upon ourselves a status lower than that which was ascribed to us by our Creator?

He deemed you far more than a dog or cow and because he placed such great value on the entity that is you he created you in his image and his likeness.

These words - bitch, heifer, pig, dog - are not terms of

endearment. They therefore should not be used in greeting to this woman for whom you'd probably lay your life down.

These words were created for specific entities; un -human entities. We were made higher than the animals and given dominion over them. Why then should we answer to bitch or to heifer with smiles on our faces?

Please, understand who you are. Internalize it. You are a human being, created in the image and likeness of a God who gave you dominion over the things which you seek to liken yourself to.

Fearfully & Wonderfully Made

To My Old Fashioned Sister

In a previous letter you may have noted a conversation between a less traditional sister and I; a letter which noted that the reason for her singleness may be the dissonance between her traditional values and the realities of being a woman living in the 21st century.

I think the key to understanding our conversation is to understand that it was a critique of abiding in this particular zone of dissonance and not a critique of traditionalism.

Having said this, I want you to know that I respect your decision to hold to the tenets of traditionalism. I don't think it makes you any less of a woman. I don't think it makes you any less educated or enlightened. I see it simply as you making a choice to travel life's course using a particular vehicle; one different from the one that I may choose.

I genuinely believe that you bring to the table a philosophy about life and living that I, as a more modern woman do not bring to the table. I genuinely believe that there are men who would love to be your traditional half. So be you without any apologies or any fear of being looked down upon.

A Modern Woman

Dear Step-Mommy,

The fruit of his loins isn't going anywhere and neither is their mother.

If you are choosing to love him then you are choosing to love his seed. If you are making the choice to respect him, then you are also making the choice to respect those whom he offered parts of himself to.

When he spilled his seed into the oracle of that woman, he declared boldly that she was to become a part of him; that they were to become one in the combination of them that is this child.

It is asking for a lot, but it is the truth of what you are getting into. If you don't think that you're big enough to manage these things, then now is the time to bow out.

Too many children suffer because some of us cannot be selfless enough to place their needs above ours. Too many children suffer over the disrespect we confer on to the women who birthed them. Please, let us make it one less.

You have not become diminished in my eyes if you think that the burden is too great to bear. It is not an easy yoke. It is not for the faint of heart and only a few can walk this journey with steps of grace. You are still very much a phenomenal woman.

To those of you who have examined the environment and still endeavor to brave it, I applaud you. I salute you. I pray more grace for you. You are phenomenal.

Another Sister

Dear Sister,

I recently watched a series called The Book of Negroes. It was mind altering to say the least. I was sharing with a friend how this television show changed my perspective on the black man as well as the black woman.

'Tis true what George Satanya said, "Those who cannot remember the past are condemned to repeat it."

After seeing a re-enactment of some of the things which our forefathers and foremothers endured, I felt it necessary to not be so hard. Instead, I saw it necessary to castigate a little less. I saw it necessary to add another dose of love to the love that I already have for my brothers and sisters.

I saw men who were forced to leave the women who brought forth their children for months on end at a time with no call and no provision. I saw men who subconsciously over compensate for the manhood that was stripped from their forefathers.

I saw men who place emphasis on ownership of the things that society deems manly as opposed to the things that truly constitute manhood: the possession of a woman and children, and seed across many plantation houses in the stead of commitment, loving, being faithful and staying when times are rough.

I saw women who are caustic, justifiably angry and justifiably bitter. I saw women who cannot and refuse to even think of allowing a man - a woman - or anyone to take care of them. We say that they're feminists. But really and truly this is what society constituted as black womanhood: never having the security and stability of the love or provision of anyone , and so it becomes necessary to do for you and yours.

True, many men and women of our generation NEVER experienced the version of slavery that their forefathers and foremothers did. But it is undeniable that some of the negative habits from that time were passed on from generation to generation.

True, we didn't experience being raped and beaten on the plantation nor did we experience the separation of our families by the slave master, but somewhere along the line called the past it happened to ONE of us, and that's all it took. That extra dose of love has nothing to do with me. That extra dose of love has to be God. Only God can right how deeply we were wronged and only God can change mindsets, and inadvertently cultures. In the stead of us castigating one another, let us take the time to bring God into the picture by loving each other a little harder.

Loving A Little More

YOU ARE
ENOUGH

Dear Rejected,

Let me tell you: I hate the word No. Plain and simple.

This is a two-letter word, which when used correctly can wreak havoc on minds, can cause the strongest souls to crumble and can destroy the most sturdy of hearts. This is a two-letter word which can cause you to question the very essence of your existence. This is a two-letter word which can chop down the faith of giants and plant the root of bitterness in their hearts. It's two letters seated right next to each other in the English alphabet, N and O, in that specific order. But it is a dangerous word. It is a humbling word. It is a hated word, and you probably hate it too.

After all, it's the word that prevented you from getting the job that you worked and studied so hard for. It's the word which prevented you from getting into the school that you wanted to get into. It's the word which the doctor uttered when you asked him if there was a cure for your Grandpa's illness. It's the word which manifested when you prayed tirelessly to God to heal your mom; to not let her die but she died anyway.

I hate the word No. And you hate it too. So why am I talking about dealing with it?

14 days ago, I celebrated my 26th birthday. For me birthdays are not so much a time of celebration as they are a time of reflection. For me they are a time to reflect on the grace and mercy of God and where I would be without them. They are an opportunity to take stock of how far I've come and how much farther I have to go.

On the morning of the 18th of March, I did just that.

I took stock.

I noted that 26 had brought a softer, more prudent me.

I noted that while I had grown remarkably in patience that I probably needed to grow some more.

I noted that I am stubborn as hell and that I have a strong grasp of what I want out of love, life and business.

I noted that I was becoming a woman that I love.

I noted that I had come into a place of maturity where I was once childish.

Hell, I even asked myself, "Chadia when did you get to be this grown? When did you get to be so remarkable - not just in the things that people see- but the person that everyone doesn't always get to see?"

Reflecting on an experience a few days prior also left me noting that 26 was probably the year to learn to deal better with rejection.

Rejection? What do you know about rejection?

Girl, I am a walking poster child for rejection. Man, the very first guy that I liked didn't like me back. Do you know what that does to an 11-year old girl who takes herself too seriously?

Umm... it turns her into a major player who breaks hearts but never gets hers broken?

But seriously, I've been rejected before. And it hurts. It stings. It burns. And it makes me mad as hell.

I've applied for a scholarships that I got rejected for. I've been loyal to friends who took my loyalty and spat it back in my face. I am constantly reminded of how decrepit of a Christian woman I am - something that is such a core part of who I am - because I have dared to believe that my womanhood does not restrict me to being an ornament in some man's home. As an entrepreneur, my services and products have been refused and a few days before my birthday I got a "No" that I didn't like.

As I've grown in age, I've learnt to cope with the difficulties and disappointments of life but rejection always shakes me to my core. I can't say that I've mastered the art of dealing with No, but because I've purposed to deal with it differently than the destructive ways in which I've dealt with it in times past, I've learnt to deal with it to get the best possible outcomes.

So how'd I deal with it?

When one ventures into deal making or management, in addition to knowing who you're "dealing" with it is important for one to know one-self. You must know who you are. You must know your strengths and weaknesses. You must know the things which trigger you and the things which can NEVER get a rise out of you. And if you do, you are in a position to manipulate your circumstances, your environment - and in this case, a No - to your full advantage.

So it shouldn't surprise you that when I decided to deal with this monster that had wreaked havoc on my life for the past 15 years that I decided to examine me. If I'm going to deal with this thing, what are the things that make me tick? Why do I behave as I have behaved? What do I feel? How do particular circumstances affect me?

If I am to explore a truthful assessment of who I am, it will reveal that I am type-A. I am highly goal-oriented, and I'm also ridiculously competitive. Most things that I undertake, I undertake with the intention of being the BEST or one of the BEST. I work hard and I work passionately, and though I rarely play, I love hard and I love passionately.

To surmise it all, I have defined myself by my ability to do almost anything that I undertake, well. I have defined myself by how well and often I win at anything: love, life, academics, games. And so there is something about rejection that does not sit well with how I've defined my self. If things are done well, if things are at their absolute best why would someone not want these things; covet these things?

And so, rejection has often baffled me and played on my fears of failing.

Rejection says, "You are not good enough" even though you've given your absolute best. Rejection says, "You are not chosen." Rejection says, "No matter how good you are, I don't want you." Rejection ignores our very makeup by denying us the love, acceptance and fellowship that we were created for. Rejection attacks your very existence - your very reason for being: purpose. It says, "You are of no value to me. You are useless to me in this or that regard. You have no use here. You have no purpose here." And so it baffles me and upsets me.

This is the answer! The thing which baffles and upsets me provides clues to the answer of how we deal with it better. We deal with it better by understanding that no matter the circumstance that we are enough.

True. To the shallowness of men our degrees may not be enough, the length of our hair may not be enough, our skin tone may be too dark or too light; we may not speak well enough. But the shallowness of man does not take away from our inherent sufficiency.

The shallowness of man does not invalidate that we were fearfully and wonderfully made in the image of God. The shallowness of man does not take away that we are enough.

In the event that it does, it is a clarion call for us to re-examine what measures we use to weigh our usefulness. In the event that it does, it is a clarion call for us to examine how and what we define ourselves by. It is a clarion call, for the simple immutability that we are always enough.

You are enough. I am enough. We are enough. Even when rejected.

Dealing With Rejection

Dear Miss Sufficient,

Please. I beg of you, do not construct misrepresentations of yourself for the sake of snatching a man. Give him the credit that his humanity deserves.

Give him enough credit to let him love you in spite of. He is not a rodent nor is he a wild animal. You do not need to dangle bait before him nor do you need to set a trap before him. He has the ability to think, to feel and to make choices.

You can't cook. Your cleaning game isn't on par and the only thing you do well in the sphere of domesticity is laundry. To some, these characterizations make your desire to be someone's wife illegal, but this is far from the truth.

There is someone who will appreciate your love for doing laundry and your ability to shape his life with your words. There is someone who will appreciate your drive and ambition. There is someone who will choose to love you for you.

This is not to say that you should not continue to grow and learn and change. This is not to say that there are no habits or traits of yours which need to be eliminated. This is not to say that you are perfect.

This is to say that someone will choose to love you anyway. This is to say that THE deity loves you, anyway. This is to say that you are enough. This is to say that you being loved is not dependent on your ability to be a domestic goddess. This is to say that your womanhood is not compromised by your inability to do some of the things which are so tied to society's definitions of womanhood. This is to say that you are enough, my beautiful sister!

The truth is there are not enough hours in a day to allow you to become everything for anyone. So be you. Be satisfied that you are enough. Be satisfied that you are ever evolving and growing. Be satisfied that you are loved by Love.

From,
Knowingly Sufficient

You've been dreaming of her since you were 15 years old: a gorgeous little girl with your head of hair and her daddy's smile. You dreamt of all the cute, pink, frilly outfits that she was going to wear from birth to a year. Then you imagined her holding on to your legs as you dropped her off for her first day of kindergarten. You thought of mini spa dates, matching pajamas, popcorn and movies in bed. Then you imagined your mini-me wearing the same dresses and hairstyles with you.

You've been dreaming of him since you met his daddy; chocolate colored skin, a mega-watt smile and the infamous bowed legs. You dreamt of all of the family portraits where you all wear matching colors and shoes. You imagined dropping him off on his first day of kindergarten, talking to him about his first girlfriend, and reluctantly letting him go when he makes the decision to leave and cleave.

Today, you're 30 years old and you've been happily hitched for a couple of years. You believe that the time is ripe for the conversion of dream into reality. You have no idea if you're going to get a rambunctious little boy or that little girl that you've dreamt of for years. But whatever the Lord is willing to give, you'll gladly take. You're simply ready to make your foray into motherhood. You're ready to see mini versions of yourself and your hubby running around.

6 months into your attempts to begin the journey of motherhood, nothing has happened. You and hubby are enjoying the process but at this stage, you're ready for the end. You're ready to hear that you're with child. You'd even happily endure a few weeks of morning sickness. But hey, you've heard that it takes some time for a few people. Maybe you just need to make a few adjustments to your diet. Maybe you've neglected some supplements that you should be taking. Maybe you need some advice.

You and hubby make a visit to the doctor. A barrage of tests and three weeks later, you all find out the news that floored you. A barrage of tests and a few weeks later they tell you that your womanhood cannot fulfill its promise of motherhood.

Dear Sister,

That last line? I believe that they got it all wrong. I believe that by virtue of being woman that you have within your divine embodiment the capability of becoming mother.

Yes. Naturally, your womb or your fallopian tubes have denied your entrance to the door. But I believe that these organs are only natural manifestations of the divine embodiment of womanhood. I believe that while they provide a path of entry into motherhood, that they do not a mother make. I believe that there are other ways to make your foray into motherhood.

Yes. They may not be the combination of chromosomes that you initially planned on. But I think ultimately that motherhood is about being an extension of God to those who need it. I believe that ultimately motherhood is about guiding, correcting, disciplining, loving, caring and a capacity to give of oneself in unmentionable ways.

Sister, do not for a moment believe that this letter seeks to trivialize or invalidate your pain. I think that I may not understand it as well as someone who's already walked in your shoes. But I think I somewhat understand the disappointment that comes with wanting something that you have been taught should rightfully be yours yet being denied it.

I'm definitely not saying, "Don't cry". I'm definitely not saying, "Get over it." Amidst your pain and disappointment, I simply seek to provide another perspective; a more hopeful perspective. Amidst your pain and disappointment, I'm here to say that you may not acquire what you dreamt of in the way that you thought you would acquire it. But, I believe that your dream is still very much attainable.

I believe that there are little girls who've been denied it, yet would love someone to have pajama parties and who would love to have mini spa-dates with someone like you. I believe that there are little boys who've been denied the hug and comfort of a mother and long for someone like you in their lives.

So definitely, cry if you must. Be disappointed if you must. But I also want you to be hopeful and be open to the idea that there are legions of motherless children waiting to become recipients of the love you hold in your heart. Most of all, I want you to know and be sure, that this experience which has birthed your disappointment does not make you any less of a woman. You are enough.

Your Sister,
Chadia

Dear Sister,

Be careful of the man who tells you that you need to fit a particular mould. Be careful of the man who tells you that if you do not speak or laugh with genteel airs that you are not yet prepared to be someone's wife.

Be careful of the man who will hold up before you another woman and tell you that you should be her; that you should hold to her ideals or that you should want to dress in the same way that she does.

Be careful of the man who believes that it is his job to fashion and shape you, unaware of, and spitefully neglecting the fact that you are not his creation.

You need not be anyone else but you, because you are enough.

Chadia

THE FIGHT

Dear Sister,

Sometimes you may fight battles and you may find the hearts of men so hardened that you will believe that your fight is futile. I've found myself here many times, but I have learnt that every battle lost is not a battle not to be fought.

For some of the battles I fight now, my grandchildren will win the war. I have began and they will finish. Some of the things which lay heavy on my heart will not change in my time but my grandchildren will experience freedoms that I didn't. So, I fight!

You may have found yourself in a situation where some people are myopic concerning some of the things which you do and say now. But if God has given you the vision, push on! If it is any consolation or encouragement, remember that Moses carried the vision of the Promised Land but did not see it. His descendants did.

It's quite possible that you may experience a similar fate.

The Fighter

Dear Sister,

Perhaps it is because I was bullied as a kid. Perhaps it's because I'm five feet and often underestimated. Perhaps, I still don't know the reason why yet, but I do know that I love a good fight. I love causes. I love freedoms. I love winning.

I love giving a voice to the voiceless. I love seeing the underdog prevail and I love fighting. But I'm learning not to fight for everything. I'm learning to fight with a little bit of wisdom.

At 26, I've learnt to stop fighting for fighting sake. I've learnt to fight for the things which matter. I've learnt that causes aren't worth fighting for if they're just for the sake of being allowed to be me; if they're for the sake of allowing human beings to simply do as they please.

It has been impressed on my heart that causes are only worthy if they allow for the full expression of the glory of God. So I fight ONLY for causes that reveal the heart of God towards humankind.

I fight for the causes that allow women to be everything that they were created to be: autonomous, free thinking, mothers, wives, single and slaying, doctors, nurses, and engineers. I fight for causes that give life in the stead of taking it away. I fight for the causes that do not encourage mere men to believe that they are as mini Gods in their homes. I fight for the causes that reflect the heart of God towards humankind. I fight for the causes that take away limits on my expression of God's glory in fullness.

I fight. But I choose to fight worthily.

Sincerely,
The Fighter

DEALING WITH THE DIVINE

Girrrlllll….

So I met a young man a few weeks ago. He was interesting enough for me to agree to go to lunch with him. Now you know that I'm incapable of small talk so it is an unspoken truth that a decision to take me to lunch is a decision to be thoroughly engaged on every topic under the sun: religion, politics, love, dating, ambitions, goals and dreams.

The conversation got off to a nice enough start. It was nice to meet a brother who was genuinely interested in digging deep; a brother who could actually hold a conversation. He had engaged me on fitness, ambitions, international politics, and goals before our conversation veered into the realm of faith. I think that within the first 3 minutes of that segment it had been well-established that I was a "poto leglise" (not really), that I hold conservative ideals about sex and marriage (I have my liberal ideals too) and that the only type of man who could consistently engage me was a God-fearing man.

But then I asked him about his faith. He said, "I'm Christian. I have sex (the brother is not married), but it doesn't interfere with my relationship with God."

I said, "Really? That's interesting." I had a mini tirade about how I am so tired of these men who claim to be God-fearing yet piss in God's eyes and call it rain and then I proceeded to throw a question at him.

I said to him, "Listen to this. If you and I were in a relationship or married and you know that there are things you do that irritate me - like leaving your shoes in the middle of the room or continually leaving your wet towel on the bed - would you not do everything in your power to stop these things out of your respect or value for me or would you come to the conclusion that this thing is irritating her, but it's not affecting our relationship so I'm just going to ignore it?"

He was silent. He knew that if he'd adopted a similar stance in a relationship with a woman that he'd probably be without a woman. He knew that if he loved a woman that he would do everything in his power to please her, to show her that she is valued, honored and respected.

I was fine with his silence. It meant that I had encouraged some thought. Since the mission had been accomplished, I politely changed the topic to safer ground and we laughed and chatted for an additional 2 hours.

But where I was done with him is not where I'm not done with you. I shared this story to point out something in particular.

Some of us treat human beings better than we treat God. We seek to please them, we study them and we cater to them, but we leave our relationship with God in neglect. It puzzles me. How can we be so mindful of the people whom we love but abuse the God who first loved us?

We'll stop leaving our shoes in the middle of the corridor at our spouse's insistence because we value them and want to live in harmony with them, yet we will ignore God's laws and precepts - God whom we say takes precedence above all - which were created for our own benefit.

We'll be sure to plan and set up date nights because we understand the importance of spending time with our significant other. Yet, we won't set aside time to talk and walk with God.

By now, you "ketch" my drift.

If you're reading this, and you've ever used the motif, "God first" as the guideline to your existence, I challenge you to truly put him first. Do the things which please Him. Love Him. Cater to Him. Listen to Him. And only then, will he truly be first.

Putting God First

Dear Sister,

The past few weeks I've spent perhaps too many hours of my time embroiled in serious trash talk on Facebook. It was NBA playoff season. Need I say more?

Lebron James, affectionately called King James is one of my favorite basketball players. Physically, he is a beauty to behold. A man of his size is perhaps better suited to the clashing associated with American football. But he's managed to carry all of this to the basketball court and when he hits the paint, he's simply unstoppable. Still, Lebron has yet to leave the mark that many, like me, expected him to leave.

On Friday evening as the Golden State Warriors beat the Cavs on their own court to move to a very favorable 3–1 lead, I shook my head. I shook my head because for another year I felt that Lebron James had disappointed me. I shook my head because for another year I felt like the King had not shown up. I shook my head because I knew that for the rest of the night I was about to be the recipient of some of the most scathing taunts by friends and acquaintances who simply couldn't stand Lebron James.

Just as I expected, the taunts came in one by one. One of the taunts encouraged me to turn away from Lebron because he had been such a disappointment; such a let down. To this, I responded that he was still King in my palace. My loyalty to this man that I'd NEVER met was astounding.

And then it got me thinking. How do I behave when I find myself in a place where God doesn't show up? Would my response carry the same brand of loyalty that it did when I spake of a mere human being?

I am in a season in my life where I am questioning many of the things which I had been taught about Christianity and God. I'm in a season where I accept things exactly as they are. I'm in a season where I've moved away from sugarcoating things for the sake of creating a more palatable pill out of the God that I serve. I've learnt to accept that no matter the outcome, He is God.

When I was growing up, I was told that God always shows up. He always answers. He's always there. Yet, in my personal experience I've sometimes felt that I was deserted. I've sometimes felt like God didn't show up for me. I've learnt that these feelings are valid. But I've also learnt that there is something more important than these feelings. What's even more important is how I deal with these feelings.

I've had experiences where I felt strongly that God had spoken to me and led me in a particular direction. I was so excited about these moments that I shared them. But the end result didn't always match my expectations. I've had experiences where people with lots of life left to live and lots of impact left to give were suddenly take from me and I felt that I couldn't justify God's Kingship. In some of these moments people taunted me and mockingly asked me, "Where is Your God?"

My responses weren't always the right ones. But I'm conscious now. So in the state of my consciousness I wonder: When people ask me , "Where is your God?" will I sill stand boldly and declare that he is still the King of My Palace; still the King of My Heart?

My experience this playoff season has taught me to say, no matter the circumstance, that God is God. If I can still see the greatness in a mere man when time and time again he has not met my expectations how can I not teach myself to see the all powerful, all knowing God with these very same eyes? How can I not teach myself to see God with these very same eyes when he is faithful to work out all things for my good

P.S. The Cleveland Cavaliers came back and emerged NBA champions that season

King James Fan (I Ain't Talking 'Bout The Bible)

Dear Sister,

We are often puzzled and disappointed when we do things according to God's plan and voice and do not experience particular blessings and benefits. It is nothing but human pride. We want to believe that something we do of our human ability can make us deserving of the goodness of God. So we work for it.

We want to believe that we snatched up a good husband because we were paragons of virtue. We want to believe that we were healed because our faith was strong enough. We want to believe that we have material things: cars, clothes and nice houses, because we were righteous and faithful.

I've come to realize that our job here on earth is not to work for the goodness of God to manifest in our lives. Our job here on earth is to display his glory even in the worst of our circumstances. We serve a sovereign God who chooses to, and will do as he pleases. He will bless who he so desires. He will heal who he so desires. He will shape and allow circumstances as he so pleases.

This is not to say not to aspire to keep His commands and tenets. This is not to say that we will NEVER receive blessings or gifts during our lifetime on earth. It's simply to remind us that all of our righteousness is as filthy rags. There is NOTHING we can do that can EVER make us righteous enough for, or deserving of the Lord's blessings. We are righteous - or rather, becoming righteous - simply because He has decided to make us righteous through the sacrifice of His son.

Don't Get It Twisted.

Dear Peace-less,

I have often been asked, "Do you have peace about it?" when I'm about to make a major decision, or say or do something. Sometimes I do, and sometimes I don't.

I've learnt that inner peace is not always the pre-requisite for determining whether what I'm going to do or say is God-ordained. I'm learning that there are times God will ask one to speak and one will have no peace. I'm learning that there are times God will ask one to go somewhere and one will have no peace about the move.

One will sense that what one will say or do will uproot, it will break walls and barriers, it will cause one to be ostracized and persecuted. In this case, there is an inner conflict not because one is not expressing the will of God but because of other factors such as: rebellion, pride and fear.

On the other hand, there are moments where moves contrary to God's desire bring a particular brand of peace because it provides the comfort and security that our flesh so often craves. We'll take a job that we shouldn't or forego the risk of moving to a new city or community when we really should. When we're guided by fear as opposed to purpose the comfortable decision always seems to be the right and peaceful decision.

Peace is to mean that there is an alignment with your spirit and God's spirit; a resignation of your spirit to the will of God. But peace can also mean: comfort, stability and security. In light of these things I think a better way of weighing if that next decision that you are about to make is the will of God is to examine why you have peace or why you don't have it as opposed to whether it's there or not.

Is it because what you are about to say and do will please man or is it because you fear man's backlash? Is it because what you are about to say is not in keeping with God's heart or is it because the timing is not right? Is it because the decision calms your anxiety? Is it because it conforms to logic and science?

This examination - to be done in deep prayer - will uncover the heart of the matter and will, in many cases, help you to find the equilibrium - the brand - of peace that we all aspire to: our will in alignment with the Lord's will. Purpose.

Chadia

Heya sis,

When the world experiences devastation and the depravity of humanity is made clear, we hear people say things like,

"What has this world come to?"

"These are not human beings. They are animals."

There is a sense of dread that those who dabble in such wicked acts - murder, terrorism, rape, debauchery, selfishness and thievery - are in some way kindred to us. We want to separate ourselves. We want to make distinctions. But the truth is that they are of our kind. Human, is exactly what they are.

The beautiful news is that there is room for separation. We can separate ourselves. Our separation is found in the expression of faith in our hearts; an expression that catapults us into the shower of God's grace; an expression that renders us "not of this world."

So... the next time an occurrence encourages you to distinguish between yourself and "this world", if you are unsaved, seize the opportunity to invite Jesus into your heart and if you have already made that declaration of faith, see it as an opportunity to bow your knees in thankfulness to the Lord for grace extended to you.

Grace Grabber

Hey girl,

A few days ago, life gifted me a big NO. I was awarded a full tuition scholarship to study Law at a university in England, and everything said that I would be going except I lost the scholarship.

I required funding from the bank to meet my visa requirements and the approval only came through 17 working days from my point of application. 17 working days was 2 working days too late. When I sent in my documents to the school I found out that they were no longer issuing CAS (a requirement for my visa application).

Me being me - I hate NOs and will do everything to convert one into a YES - I tried everything within my power to get the school to reconsider and to maybe defer my scholarship to the next term. I emailed the Dean, and the Vice Chancellor but this was just not to be my season.

The first day, I was angry and inconsolable. Those who know me will say that tears are a foreign thing to me but I spent the entire day in my room in tears. The people in my house barely laid eyes on me. I didn't eat. I sat in my room and these globs - the compound of Hydrogen and Oxygen and possibly some Sodium Chloride too - just came. At times they flowed but at other moments I sobbed.

This was something that I wanted and worked for and it was lost. Hearing anything about God during that day was just unfathomable to me. Where was he when this was going on?

By the second day I had come to terms with it. I had lost an XCD 90,000 scholarship and it wasn't coming back. Life was going to move on with or without me. So what would I do?

A few days before the No, I had written the first chapter in a book I call "Success Hacks from Jesus". The chapter is titled, "Shake the Dust Off Your Feet" and deals with the best way to deal with the inevitable Nos that life will throw at us. As I read, I couldn't help but think that I had written this for myself.

Over the days following, I would write 3/4 of the book, and I would become a book cover designer. I would also design the website for a project that I had decided that I could start a little later (Reveal coming soon) and most importantly, I'd learn from experience, not just from thought how to shake the dust off my feet and look toward success.

NO does not mean the demolition of a a bright future. It can simply mean redirection.

Redirected

Dear Sister,

Looking back at the previous letter took me back. It took me back to one of the most difficult periods of my life. Today, I can't say that I'm glad that I lost the scholarship but I think on my life and all the things that I've done since losing the scholarship and I wonder if these things would have happened if I had been in England studying Law.

Would I have still been as passionate about the Caribbean and its development as I am now? Would I have started Caribbean Entrepreneur and African Entrepreneur? Would I have started Wakonté? Would I have started #TheLettersProject? Would you be reading this book?

I don't know the answers to these questions but I do know that I am content with where I am today. I do know that I've experienced tremendous growth and I think I probably now hold a more realistic view of life. Most importantly, I think my relationship with God has definitely gone to new depths.

Even when things don't work out according to my expectations I've learnt to trust that everything will work together for my good. I've learnt to trust implicitly that God's thoughts towards me are good and greater than any dream that I could have.

So no, I can't say that I'm happy that I lost the scholarship. I can't say that I had foresight that revealed the divine blue print that said, "scholarship lost". But I am content with where I am, I value the lessons learnt from repurposed dreams and I can truthfully and joyfully say that I wouldn't re-chart the journey. Instead, I look forward to where the Lord's directions take me. I look forward to fulfilling purpose.

Seeing Through New Lens

Dear Searching One,

I sat and took in the scenes from the reel that is your life.

You seek comfort and soothing in the doldrums of a bottle, but still your pain doesn't go away.

You seek acceptance in the embrace of snakes and they do what snakes do. They poison you with venom to make the kill easier.

You burn away your insides with acid because you believe that you don't deserve to be here.

You are searching for life's purpose and life's meaning. You are searching for love, comfort and acceptance. May I be so bold as to say that I know where your search ends?

Dear Wanderer, I want to tell you that whatever it is you look for, you can find it in God: love, acceptance, forgiveness, faithfulness, kindness, comfort, joy, and peace.

I promise that you can find these things in Him. I speak of the God who loved you so much that he sent his only son to be crucified on a cross for you. I know that He loves you even when you don't love you. So run to Him.

Run to a well of never-ending water. Run in to the arms of the One who sticketh closer than a brother. Run into the arms of Love.

I Dun' Tried It

MY PRAYER
FOR YOU

Dear Sister,

I would be telling complete and utter untruths if I said that I didn't enjoy this experience. It was cathartic, it was enlightening, it was humorous and it was telling.

It was an opportunity to see how we've grown over the years. It was an opportunity to weed out our bad habits and philosophies and cultivate new ones.

Though it will take some time before I respond to your next few letters, I must note that this is not to be the end. We must do this again.

But for now, I leave you with my prayer for you.

Sincerely and Much Love,
Chadia

Dear Sister,

I wish for you the absolute best in love, in health, and in life. I pray that you encounter God in a beautiful and transformative way. I pray that you understand purpose in a deep and meaningful way. I pray that you meet the fullness of the woman that you are, and that you love what and who you see when you look in the mirror. I pray that doors of opportunity will carry you where your character can keep you, and I pray that you learn to make life's difficult decisions with grace.

I hope that you read amazing books, listen to great music, travel to life-changing places , and meet people who will remind you that there is indeed a God. I hope that you never allow yourself to be too comfortable with where you are and that you understand that while you are special, that you can always be better. And when that time comes - when you're ready for that life (chuckles) - I pray that you meet someone who understands how special you are, who will support you in your endeavors and who will love you purely. I pray that he's God-fearing, visionary and ambitious.

I hope nothing but goodness, health, love and happiness for you. But for now I gotta jet.

Much Love,
Dia

THE
ACKNOWLEDGEMENTS

So you thought that I was an ingrate, huh?

Most acknowledgements are found at the beginning of a book. But I thought it fitting that this time around the acknowledgements be placed at the end of the book. I think placing them at the end says, "I completed it, and I did it because of you."

So my acknowledgements…

It is not to be an employer of clichés that I say that I want to give the greatest of thanks to God for his faithfulness, his grace, his strength and his mercy. The past 4 years have been for me, a period where I've truly experienced the faithfulness of God. Through the ups and downs, the rain and the sun, he has kept me. My hair lost some shine, but I haven't lost my mind. I know that He is the sole reason.

My parents are deserving of many thanks. Though they often annoy me, and I am frequently looking for ways to escape their house, I don't know another couple who would, for the most part, allow me to be me. I believe that they had envisioned my path to greatness - fulfilling purpose - differently. But even when they don't quite understand what's going on (And I can't help them either because I don't always understand), they stick by me and find ways to facilitate my journey. Mummy &

Papa, thank you!

To my sister Chadel, my many cousins and supportive friends and acquaintances who believe that I will conquer every mountain or obstacle that obstructs my pathway to greatness, thank you!

To all of the writers on The Letters Project: Léel, 'Mavi, & Katrina, thank you for taking this journey with me. You poured your heart and souls out on paper and you've taken it a step further; you've decided to share it with all who want to read. Thank you for your honesty, your transparency, and your vulnerability.

To everyone who's ever bought the dream that I sold, thank you!

A big thank you to everyone who rallied to help us fulfill our crowd-funding campaign. We are eternally grateful for each and everyone of you. Still, I want to give a big shout-out to a few of the donors who have always believed in me, were there with me from the start and did not hesitate to put their money where their mouths were: DaVonne, Chelsea, Verna, Milissa, Sach, and Dr. Dede! Merci en pille!

To Damian Miles Morean, Thank you! Thank you for the many

sacrifices you made to see this through. Thank you for your patience during a difficult season. Thank you for the many encouraging conversations. Thank you for believing that I can be a Nobel Prize Winning Economist, Grammy Award Winning Artist, New York Times Bestseller and the Prime Minister of Saint Lucia all in one. You inspire me in immeasurable ways and I pray that I am even a fraction of that same inspiration to you. I know you don't like the sappy stuff, "buh is a love ting, jed". So… I love you!

To my boy B, you're always willing to come along with me on the craziest of journeys. You know what it do! For now all I can offer in return are my prayers for God's richest blessings for you and your family and continued invitations to even crazier journeys. But like I said, You know what it do… Love ya mucho!

To my brothers…

It's funny; thanking my brothers at the end of a compilation of letters that I wrote to my sisters. But as I sit back and read, sometimes with smirks on my face, I recognize that I wouldn't have written as many of the things that I wrote if I had not experienced you: the good and the bad, the patriarchy, the misogny and the love. Because of your presence, your philosophies, your rejection, your love and your acceptance, you created the perfect storm - the perfect tug of war - and you forced me into a place where I was bent on discovering God's heart for me. And I did. I recognize that it was good for me to be afflicted by the thorn that you can sometimes be. Thank you for your presence in my life!

To Life, thank you for being the greatest teacher. Thank you for teaching me humility. Thank you for throwing the curveballs that have strengthened my agility and flexibility in ways unimaginable. Thank you for helping me to see the things that I didn't know were in me.

Thank you!

Made in the USA
Middletown, DE
10 January 2022

58347585R00089